The Gig Bag Book of
GUITAR
COMPLETE

A reference guide to scales, arpeggios, and chords in all keys. A must for *all* guitarists, beginning to intermediate to advanced.

Compiled by Mark Bridges

W9-BLB-998

Cover photography by Randall Wallace
Project editor: Ed Lozano
Interior design and layout: Mark Bridges

Order No. AM 971388
US International Standard Book Number: 0.8256.1897.5
UK International Standard Book Number: 0.7119.8975.3

Exclusive Distributors:
Music Sales Corporation
257 Park Avenue South, New York, NY 10010 USA
Music Sales Limited
8/9 Frith Street, London W1D 3JB England
Music Sales Pty. Limited
120 Rothschild Street, Rosebery, Sydney, NSW 2018, Australia

Printed in the United States of America by
Vicks Lithograph and Printing Corporation

Contents

Contents

Contents

Introduction

This book is a reference guide for guitarists. It is not intended as a method book, but rather as a reference book of scales, arpeggios and chords that are easily accessible to the beginner or advanced guitarist. Regardless of your musical interest, this book contains the majority of scales, arpeggios and chords you will encounter in most styles of music (rock, jazz, country, or blues). Strong knowledge of scales, arpeggios and chords will help build familiarity with the fretboard and help develop flexibility in solo, accompaniment or ensemble playing.

The Gig Bag Book of Guitar Complete has been designed with the player in mind. You don't have to break the spine of the book to get it to stay open and it doesn't take up all the space on your music stand. It is easy-to-carry and easy-to-use. We hope that this book will serve as a valuable reference source during your years as a developing guitarist.

How to Use this Book

It is strongly recommended that you develop a practice regimen in which you devote some time to daily study. If you practice one hour each session, then devote fifteen or twenty minutes to scale, arpeggio and chord study. Another approach would be to practice your warm-up exercises with a different scale or arpeggio type each day.

Here are some helpful tips:

• Use the handy thumb index to find the key you're looking for.

For Scales:
• At the top of each left-hand page you will find the scale type and to the right you'll find the scale formula (W=whole-step, H=half-step, m3=minor third).
• Notice there are two suggested scale types along with their fingerings. (The scale types and fingerings are only suggested guidelines; you are encouraged to develop your own scale types and fingerings.)
• The scales are written in both standard notation and *tablature*. You will find a fretboard diagram in the middle of the page displaying the scale pattern (the root of the scale appears as a circle while the other scale tones appear as black dots) over the entire fretboard.

For Arpeggios:
• Notice there are two suggested arpeggio types along with their fingerings. (The arpeggio types and fingerings are only suggested guidelines; you are encouraged to develop your own arpeggio types and fingerings).
• Each variation begins on the root or fifth degree of the chord.
• The arpeggio types are written in both standard notation and tablature. You will find a fretboard diagram in the middle of the page displaying the arpeggio pattern (the root of the arpeggio appears as a circle, while the other arpeggio tones appear as black dots) over the entire fretboard.

Chord Frames

The frames used to illustrate the chords are very easy to read. The frame depicts a portion of the guitar's fretboard. The horizontal lines represent the strings of the guitar with the thickest strings at the bottom and the thinnest strings at the top. The vertical lines represent the frets. The nut of the guitar is represented by the thick vertical bar at the left of the diagram. The dots that appear in the frames illustrate where you should place your fingers. An **X** indicates that the string should be muted or not played while an **O** indicates that the string should be played open. Above each chord grid you will find the name of the chord and to the right you'll find the chord spelled out on the treble staff. Each chord type has several variations that extend the length of the fretboard. Each variation is presented from the lowest position on the neck to the highest position on the neck.

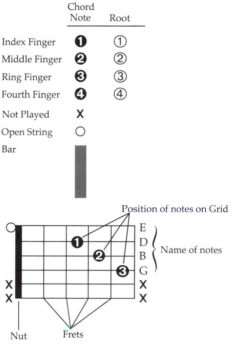

The scales presented in this book can also be found in *The Gig Bag Book of Scales for all Guitarists*. The arpeggios presented in this book can also be found in *The Gig Bag Book of Arpeggios for all Guitarists*. The chords presented in this book can also be found in *The Gig Bag Book of GuitarTab Chords* where over 2100 chord variations are presented. As with all books in *The Gig Bag series*, this book can be used as a valuable stand alone reference or enhanced by other titles in the series.

Whether you are looking to develop *chops* (technique) or broaden your scale, arpeggio and chord vocabulary, *The Gig Bag Book of Guitar Complete* is for you.

C

C major (Ionian)

WWHWWWH

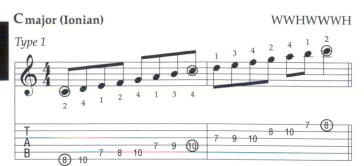

Type 1

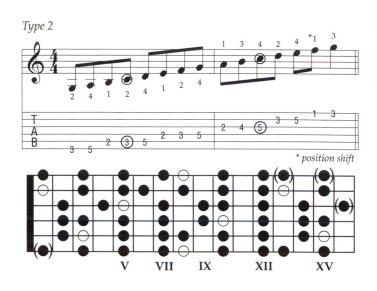

Type 2

* *position shift*

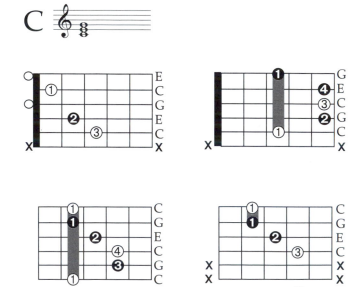

V   VII   IX   XII   XV

Cmaj7

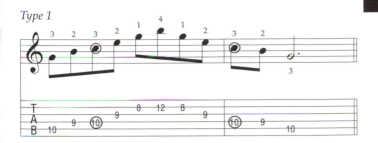

C

Type 1

Type 2

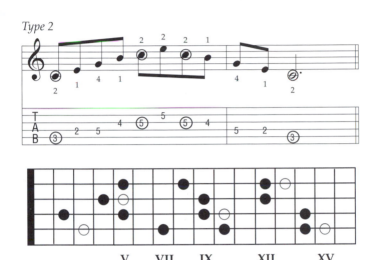

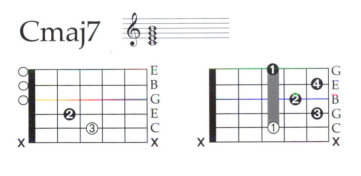

V   VII   IX   XII   XV

Cmaj7

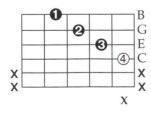

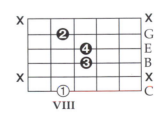

C natural minor (Aeolian)

WHWWHWW

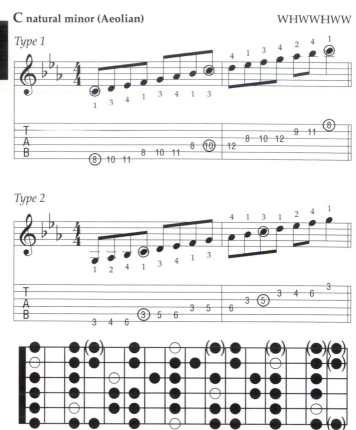

Type 1

Type 2

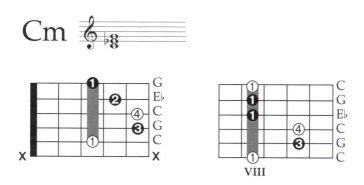

V   VII   IX   XII   XV

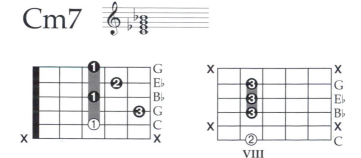

Cm

G
E♭
C
G
C

C
G
E♭
C
G
C

VIII

Cm7

G
E♭
B♭
G
C

G
E♭
B♭
C

VIII

C

Cm

Type 1

Type 2

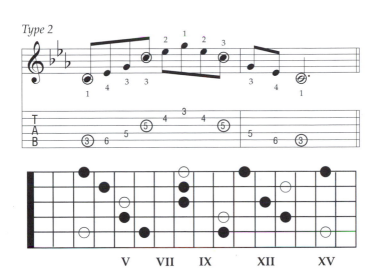

| V | VII | IX | XII | XV |

Cm add9

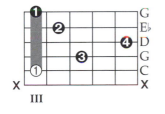

III

G
E♭
D
G
C

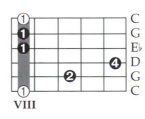

VIII

C
G
E♭
D
G
C

Cm9

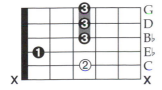

G
D
B♭
E♭
C

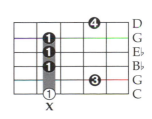

D
G
E♭
B♭
G
C

C harmonic minor

WHWWHm3H

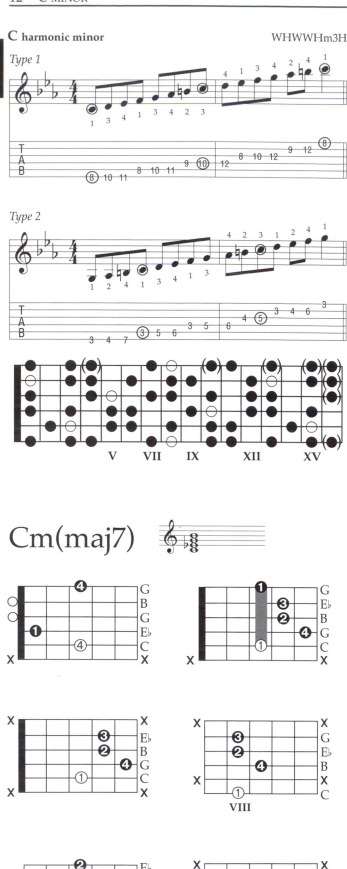

Cm(maj7)

Cm(maj7)

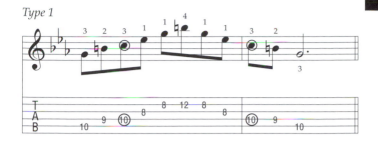

C

Type 1

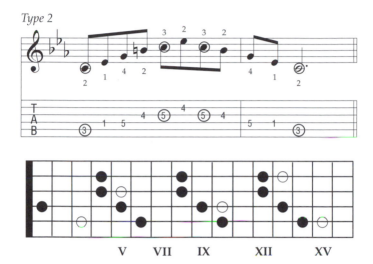

Type 2

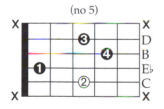

| V | VII | IX | XII | XV |

Cm(maj9)

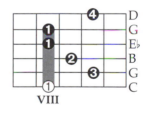

(no 5)

D
B
E♭
C

D
G
E♭
B
G
C

VIII

C jazz minor

WHWWWWH

Type 1

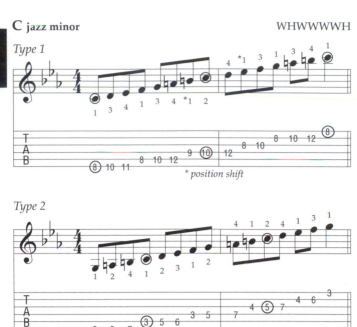

*position shift

Type 2

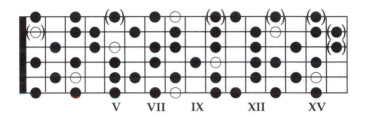

Cm6

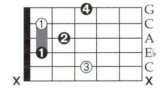

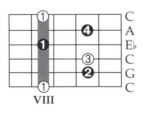

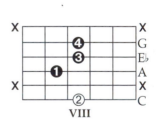

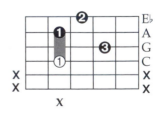

Cm6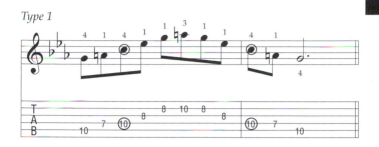

C

Type 1

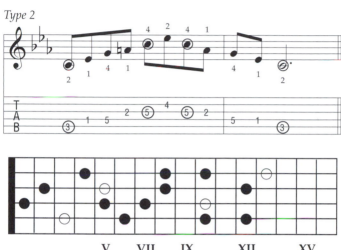

Type 2

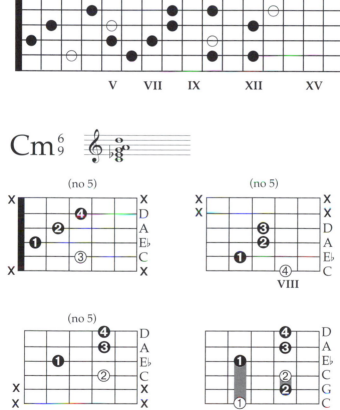

Cm⁶₉

C Mixolydian   WWHWWHW

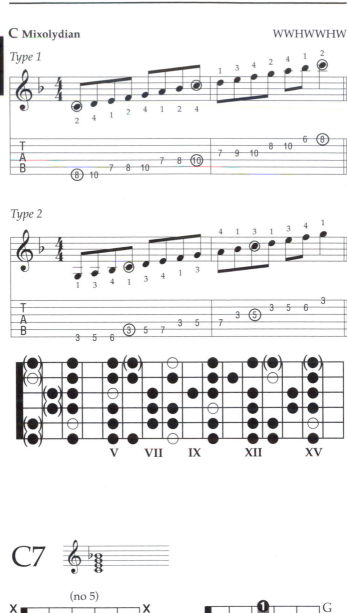

Type 1

Type 2

C7

(no 5)

C

C7

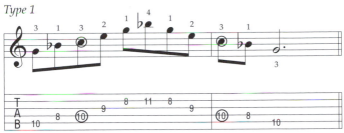

Type 1

Type 2

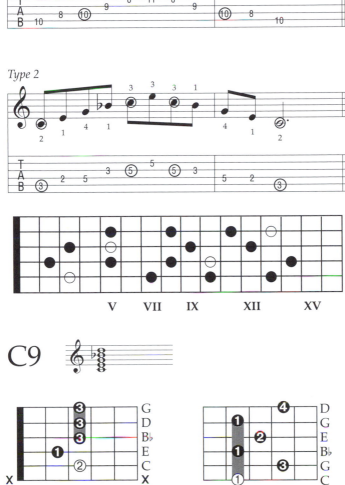

V   VII   IX   XII   XV

C9

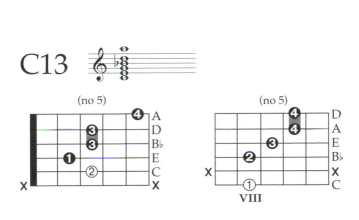

C whole tone

WWWWWW

Type 1

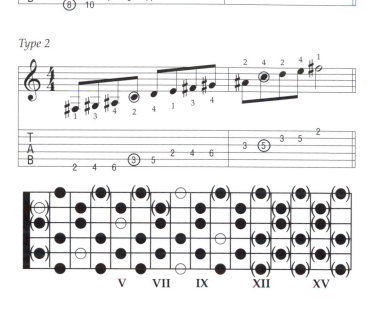

Type 2

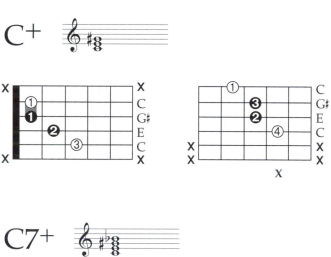

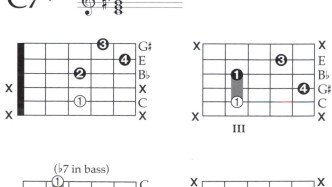

V   VII   IX   XII   XV

C+

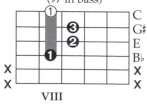

C7+

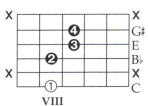

C7+

Type 1

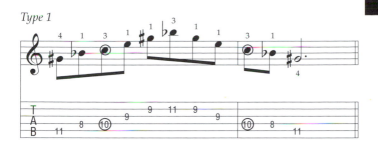

Type 2

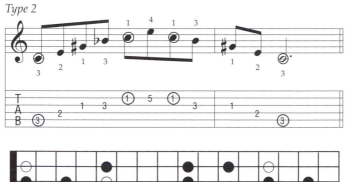

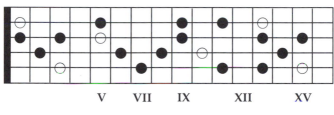

V   VII   IX   XII   XV

C7+

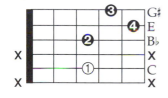

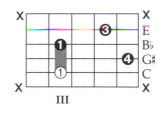

(♭7 in bass)

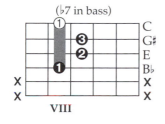

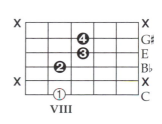

C9+

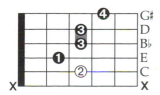

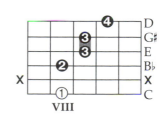

C pentatonic (major)   WWm3Wm3

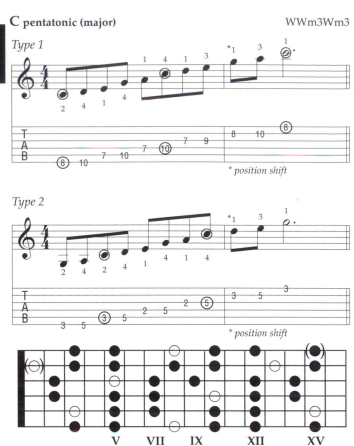

Type 1

* position shift

Type 2

* position shift

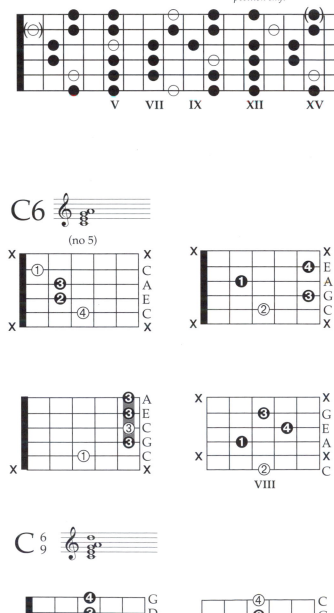

V   VII   IX   XII   XV

C6

(no 5)

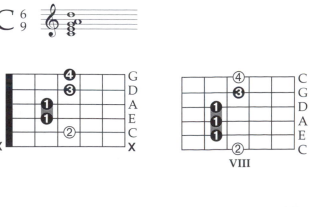

C 6/9

VIII

C6

C

Type 1

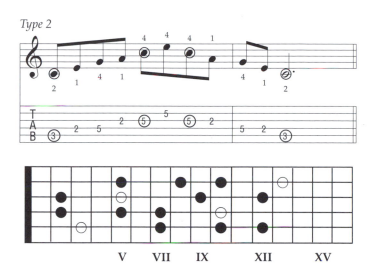

Type 2

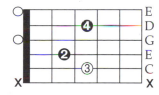

V   VII   IX   XII   XV

Cadd9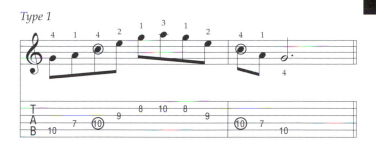

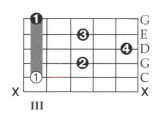

C

C pentatonic (minor)

m3WWm3W

Type 1

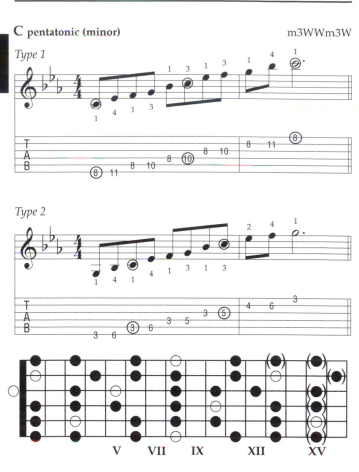

Type 2

Cm

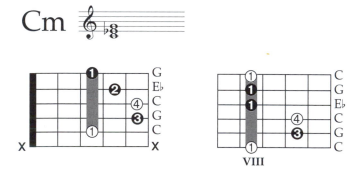

Cm7

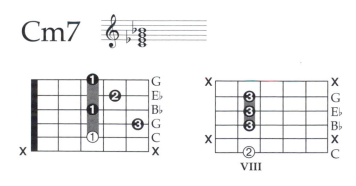

Cm7

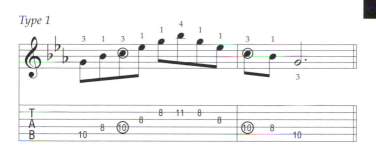

C

Type 1

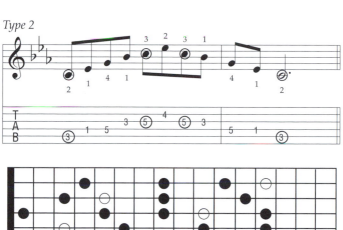

Type 2

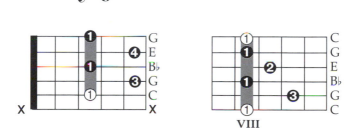

V   VII   IX   XII   XV

C7

C7#9

(no 5)

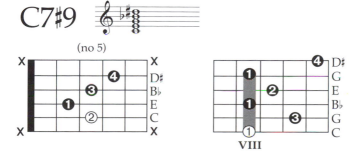

C blues scale (with major third & flatted fifth) m3HHHHm3W

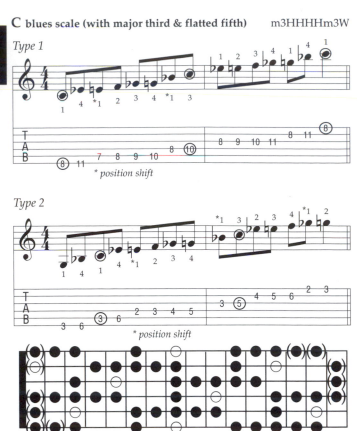

Type 1

* position shift

Type 2

* position shift

V   VII   IX   XII   XV

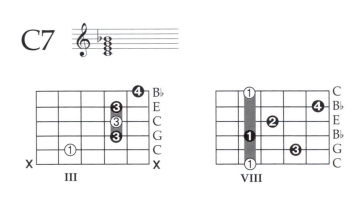

C7

III

VIII

B♭
E
C
G
C

C
B♭
E
B♭
G
C

C7♯9

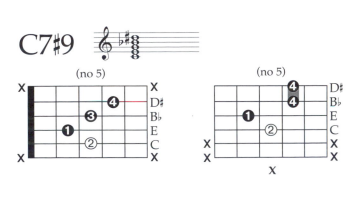

(no 5)

(no 5)

D♯
B♭
E
C

D♯
B♭
E
C

C

C7#9

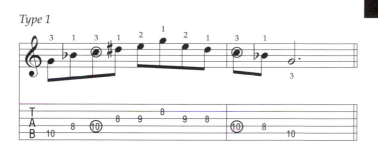

Type 1

Type 2

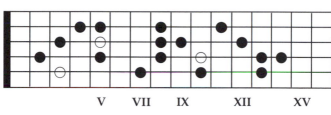

V   VII   IX   XII   XV

C9

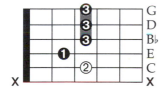

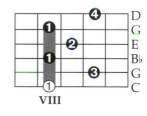

C13

(no 5)

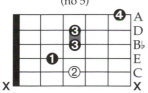

(no 5)

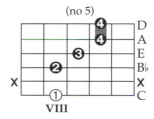

C diminished (whole-half) WHWHWHWH

Type 1

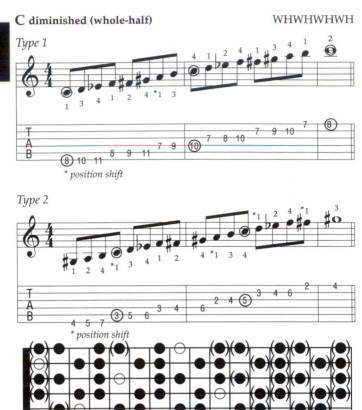

* position shift

Type 2

* position shift

V   VII   IX   XII   XV

C°

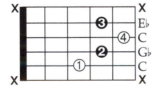

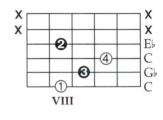

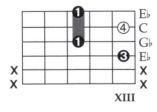

XIII

C°7

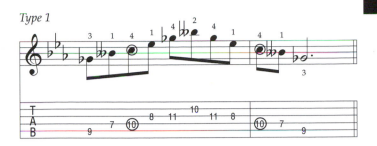

C

Type 1

Type 2

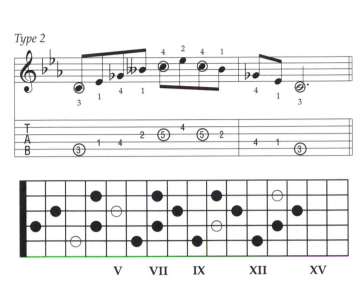

V   VII   IX   XII   XV

C°7

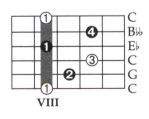

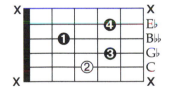

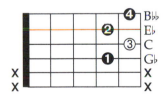

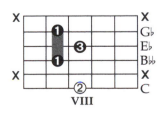

VIII

VIII

C♯/D♭ major (Ionian)

WWHWWWH

Type 1

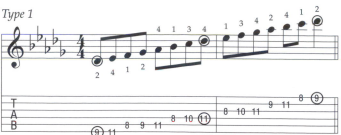

Type 2

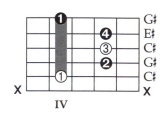

* position shift

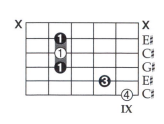

V   VII   IX   XII   XV

C♯

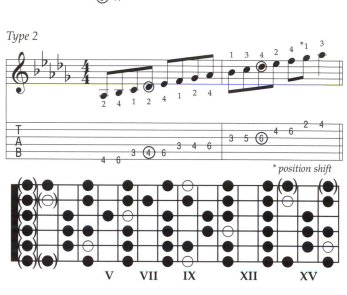

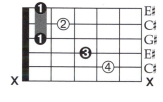

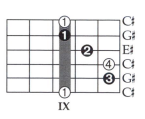

C♯maj7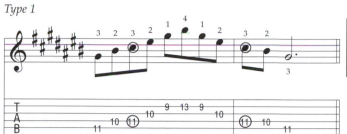

Type 1

Type 2

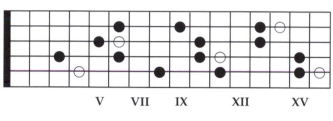

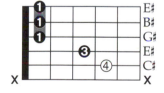

V   VII   IX   XII   XV

C♯maj7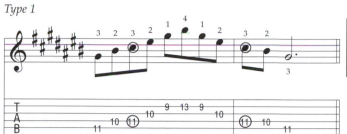

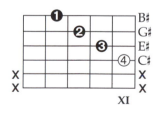

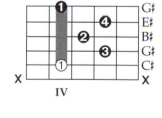

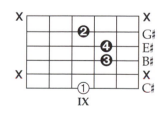

C♯/D♭ natural minor (Aeolian)

WHWWHWW

Type 1

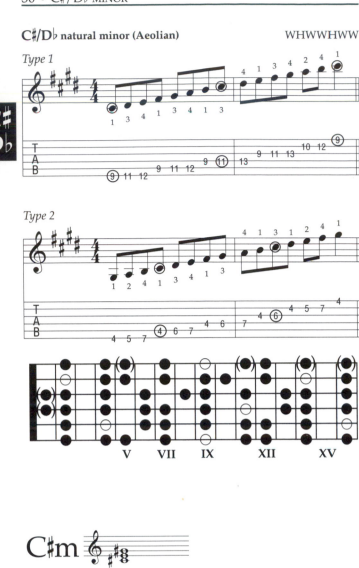

Type 2

C♯m

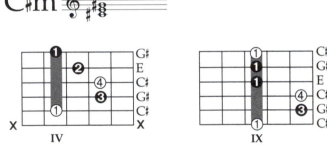

C♯m7

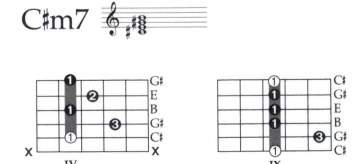

C♯m

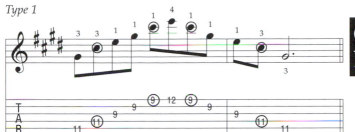

Type 1

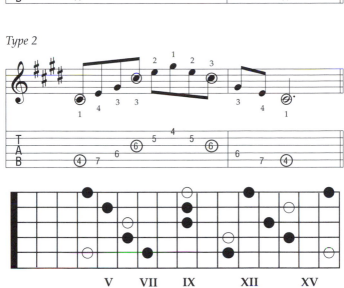

Type 2

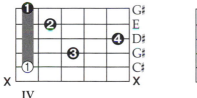

C♯m add9

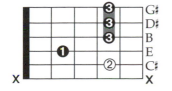

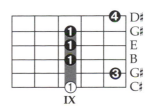

C♯m9

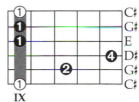

C♯/D♭ harmonic minor

WHWWHm3H

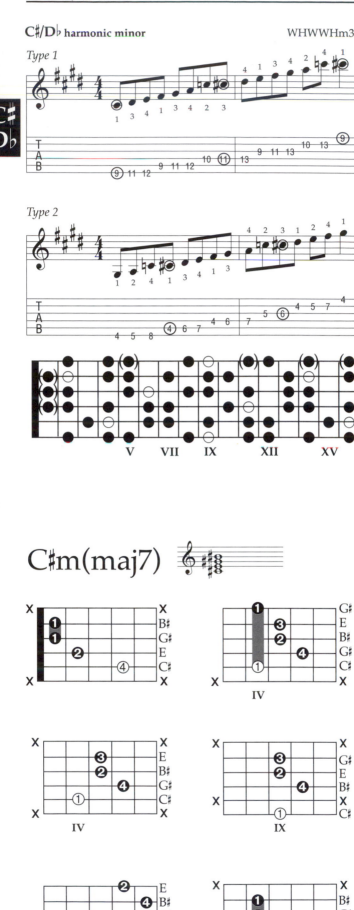

C♯m(maj7)

C#m(maj7)

Type 1

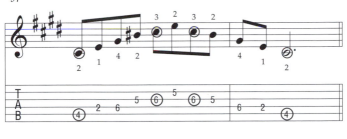

Type 2

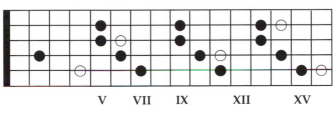

V   VII   IX   XII   XV

C#m(maj9)

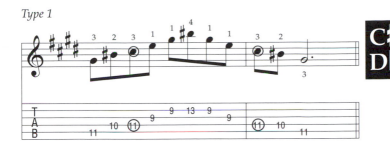

(no 5)

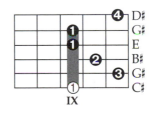

C♯/D♭ jazz minor

WHWWWWH

position shift

C♯m6

C♯m6

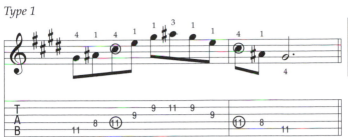

Type 1

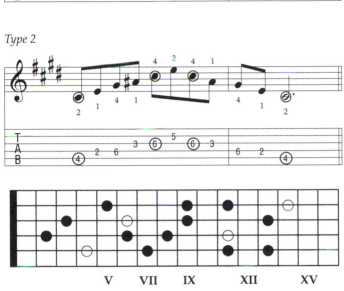

Type 2

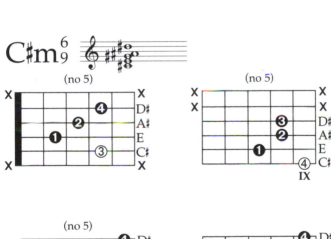

C♯m⁶₉

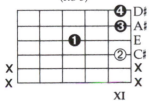
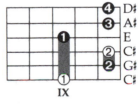

C#/D♭ Mixolydian

WWHWWHW

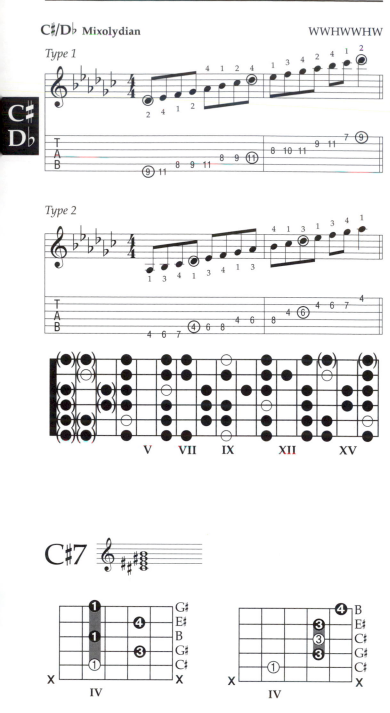

C#7

C#7

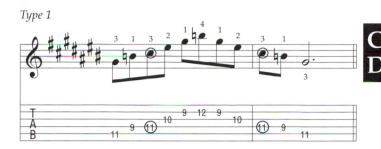

Type 1

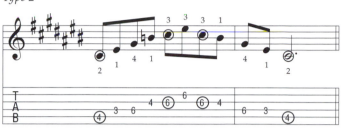

Type 2

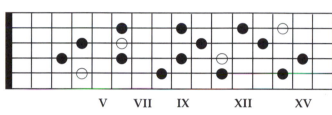

C#9

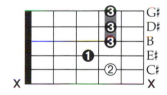

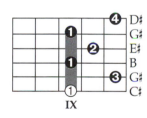

C#13

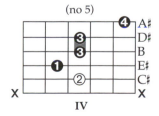

(no 5)

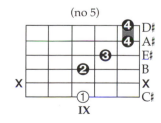

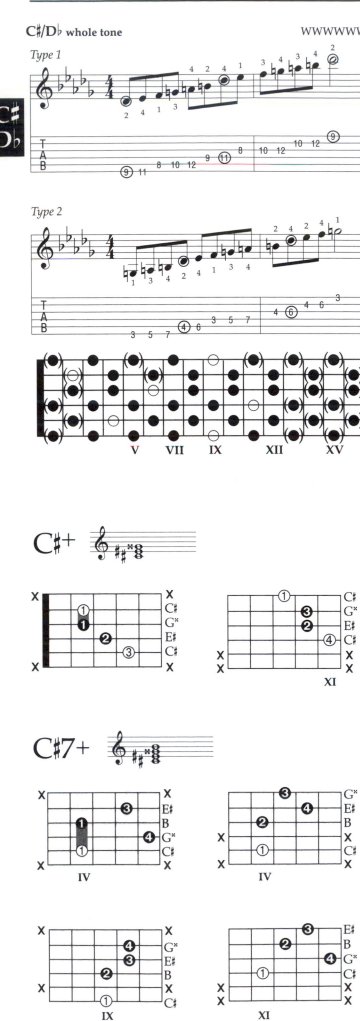

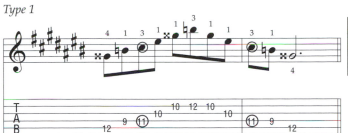

Type 1

Type 2

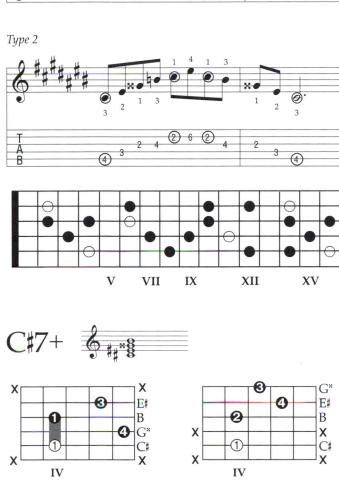

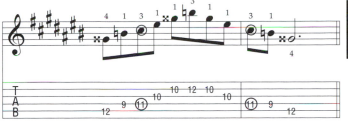

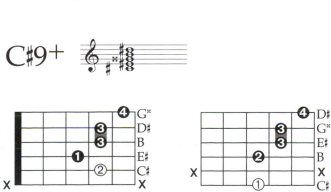

C♯/D♭ pentatonic (major)

WWm3Wm3

C♯6

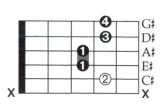

C♯⁶₉

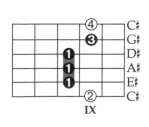

C#6

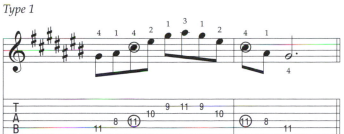

Type 1

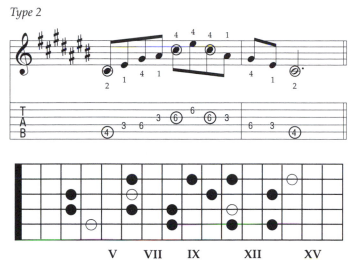

Type 2

V   VII   IX   XII   XV

C#add9

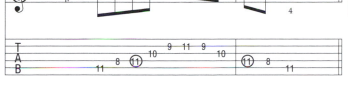

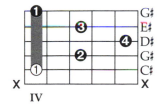

IV

G#
E#
D#
G#
C#

X   X

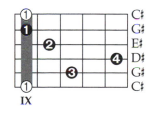

IX

C#
G#
E#
D#
G#
C#

C#/Db pentatonic (minor)

m3WWm3W

Type 1

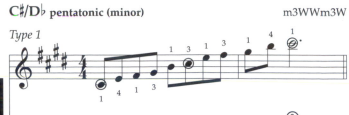

Type 2

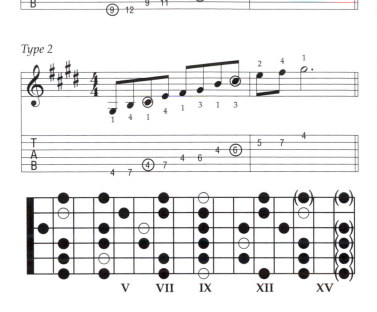

C#m

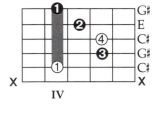

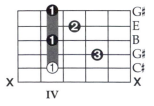

C#m7

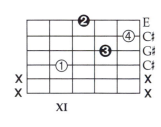

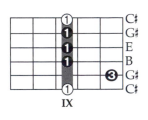

C#m7

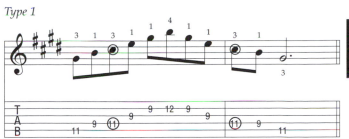

Type 1

Type 2

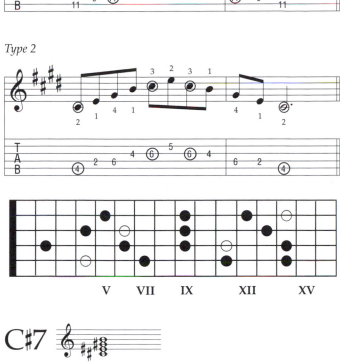

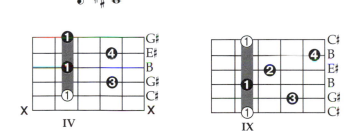

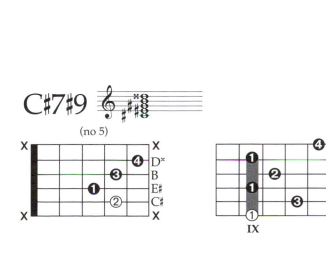

V   VII   IX   XII   XV

C#7

C#7#9

(no 5)

C♯/D♭ blues scale (with major third & flatted fifth) m3HHHHm3W

Type 1

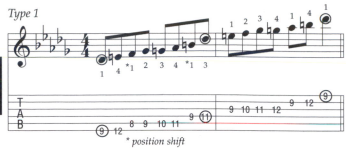

* position shift

Type 2

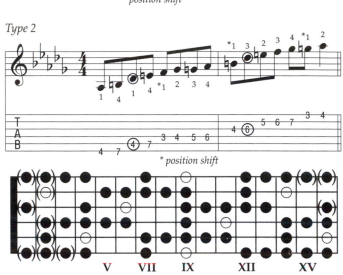

* position shift

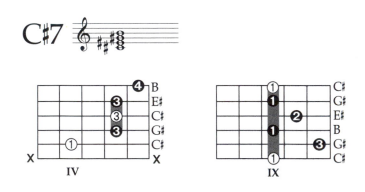

V   VII   IX   XII   XV

C♯7

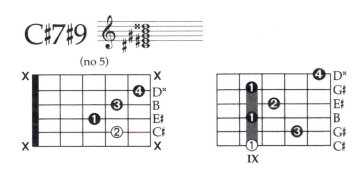

C♯7♯9

(no 5)

C#7#9

Type 1

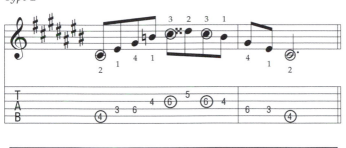

Type 2

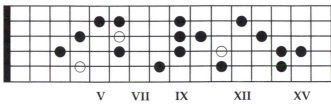

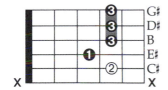

C#9

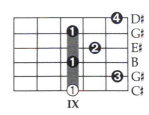

C#13

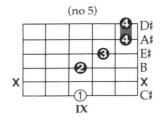

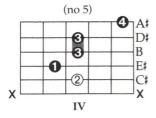

C#/D♭ diminished (whole-half)

WHWHWHWH

Type 1

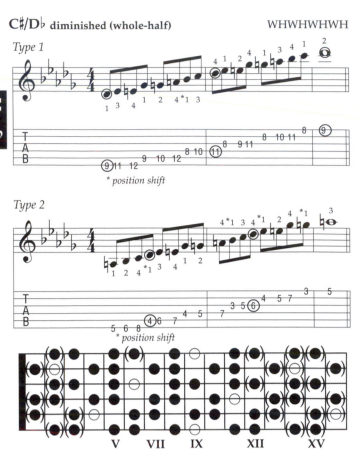

* position shift

Type 2

* position shift

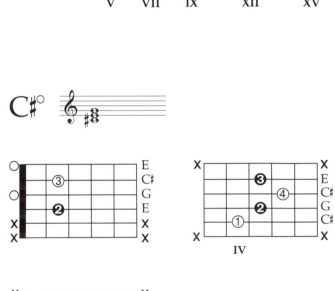

V   VII   IX   XII   XV

C#°

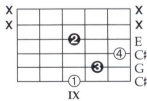

C#°7

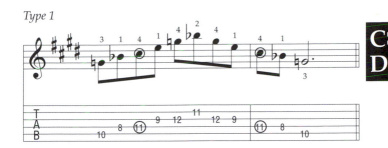

Type 1

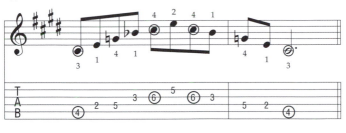

Type 2

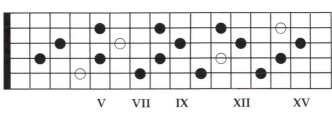

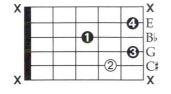

V   VII   IX   XII   XV

C#°7

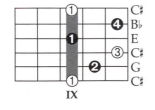

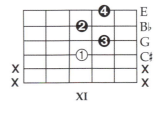

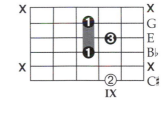

D major (Ionian)

WWHWWWH

Type 1

Type 2

* position shift

V   VII   IX   XII   XV

D

F#
D
A
D
X
X

F#
D
A
F#
D

A
F#
D
A
D
X

V

D
A
F#
D
A
D

X

Dmaj7

Type 1

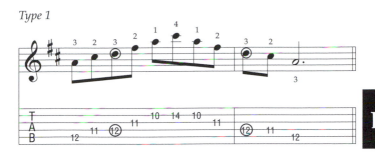

D

Type 2

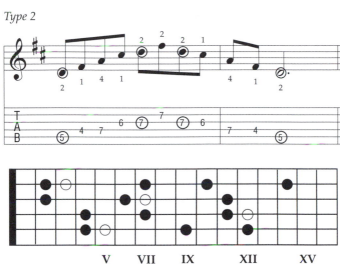

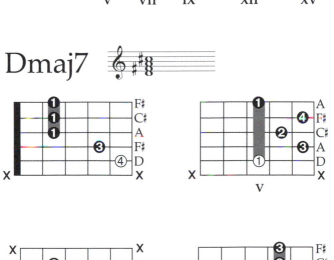

V   VII   IX   XII   XV

Dmaj7

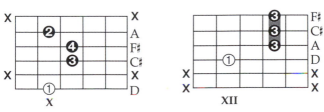

D **natural minor (Aeolian)**   WHWWHWW

Type 1

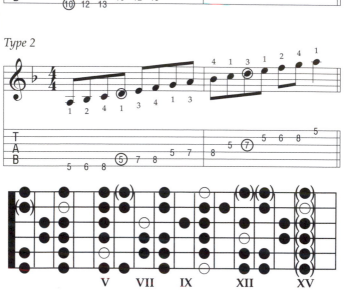

Type 2

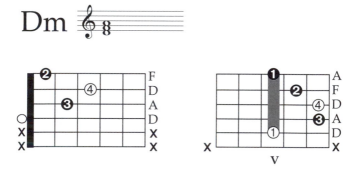

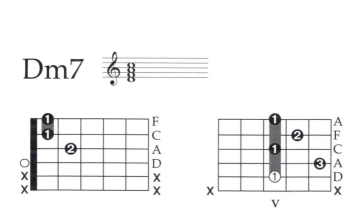

Dm

Dm7

Dm

D

Type 1

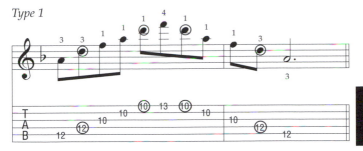

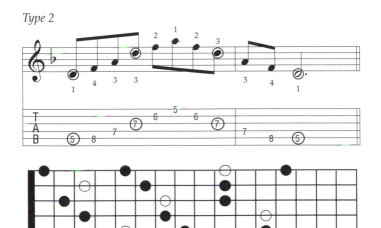

Type 2

V   VII   IX   XII   XV

Dm add9

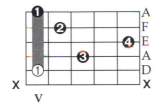

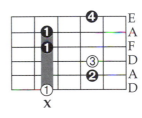

Dm9

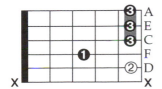

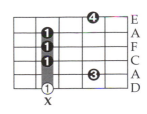

D harmonic minor

WHWWHm3H

Type 1

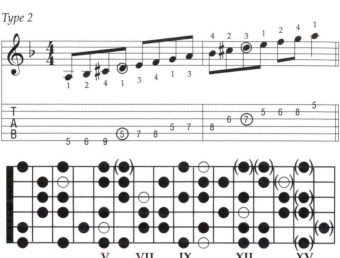

Type 2

Dm(maj7)

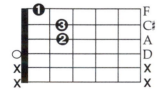

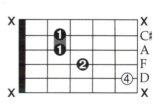

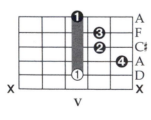

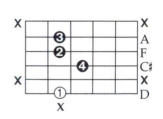

Dm(maj7)

Type 1

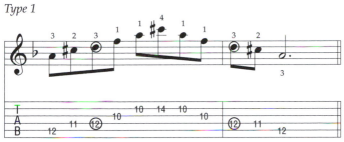

D

Type 2

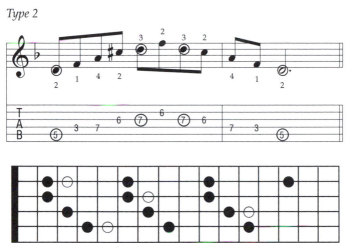

Dm(maj9)

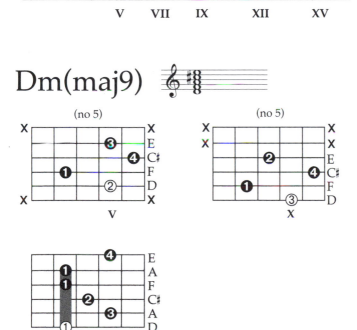

D jazz minor

WHWWWWH

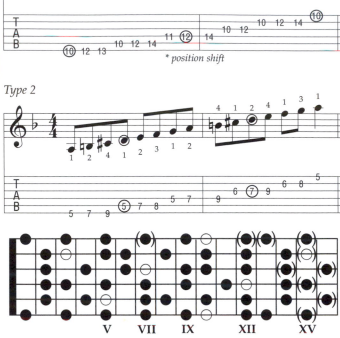

* position shift

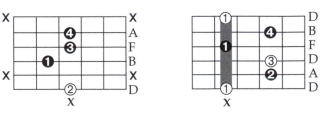

Dm6

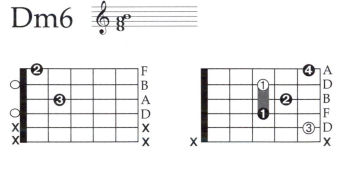

Dm6

D

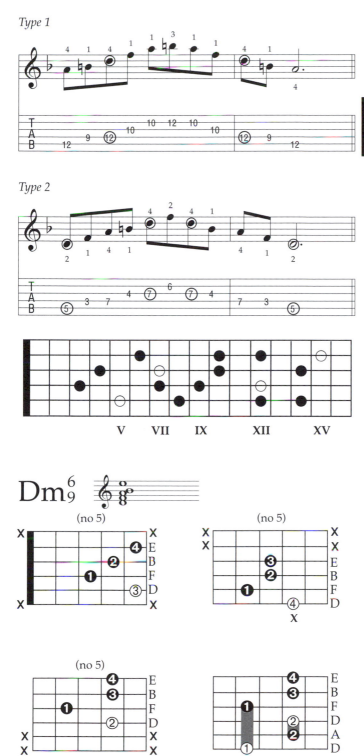

Dm$_9^6$

D Mixolydian

WWHWWHW

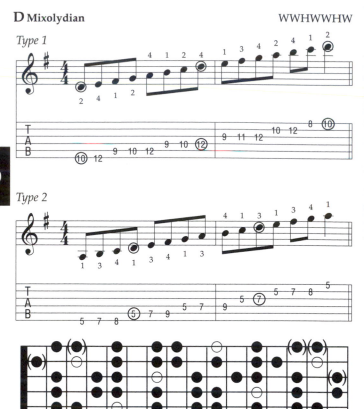

Type 1

Type 2

V   VII   IX   XII   XV

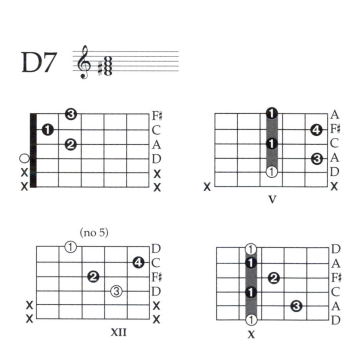

D7

D7

Type 1

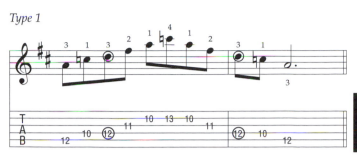

Type 2

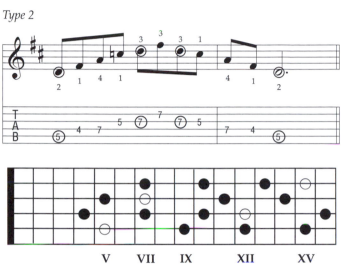

D9

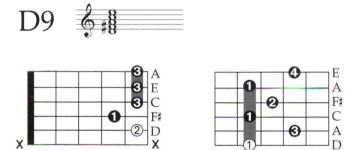

D13

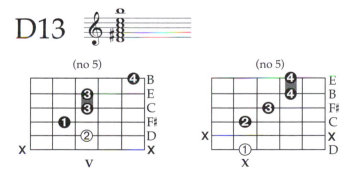

D whole tone WWWWWW

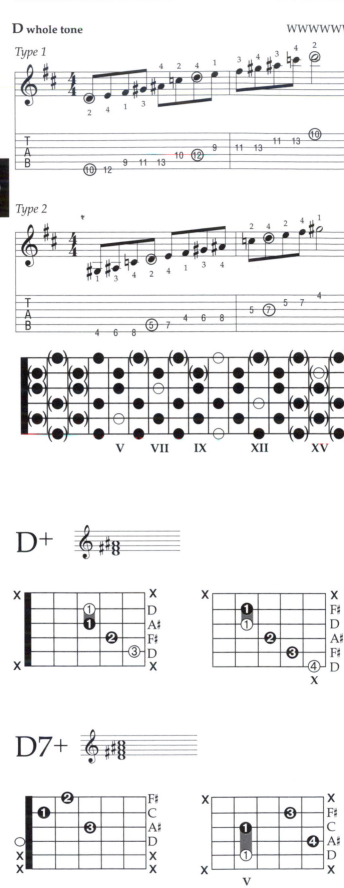

Type 1

Type 2

D+

D7+

D7+

Type 1

Type 2

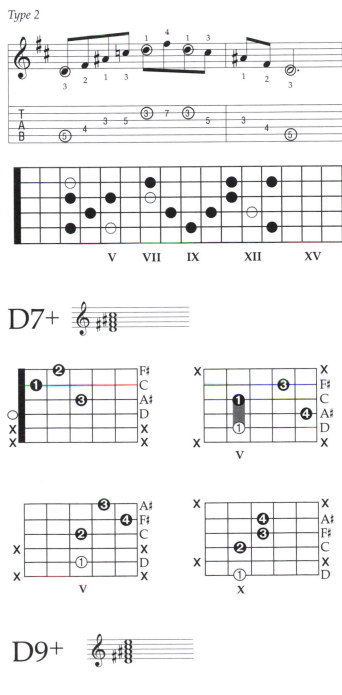

V   VII   IX   XII   XV

D

D7+

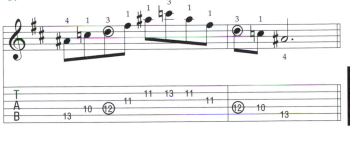

D9+

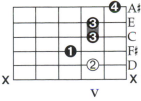
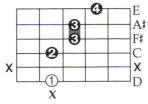

D pentatonic (major)

WWm3Wm3

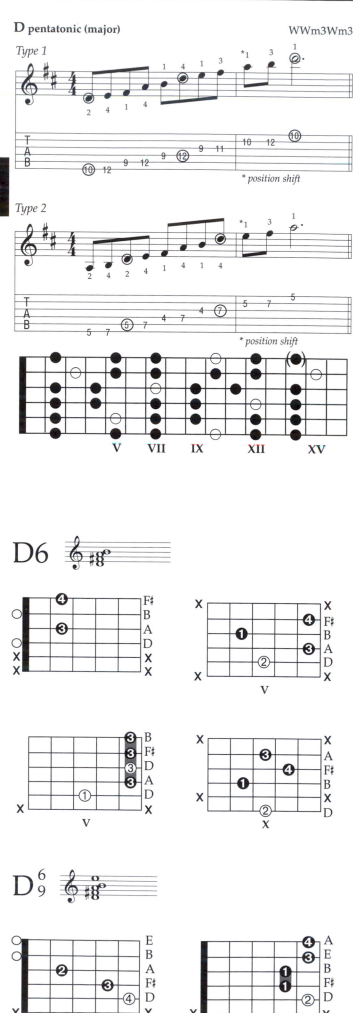

Type 1

* position shift

Type 2

* position shift

V   VII   IX   XII   XV

D6

D⁶₉

D6

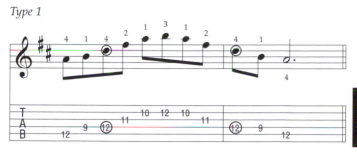

Type 1

D

Type 2

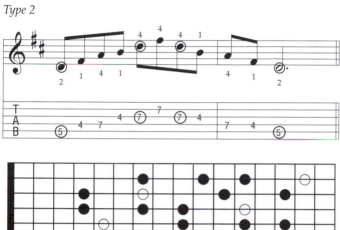

V   VII   IX   XII   XV

Dadd9

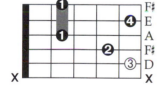

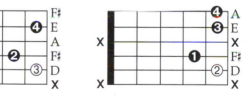

D pentatonic (minor)

m3WWm3W

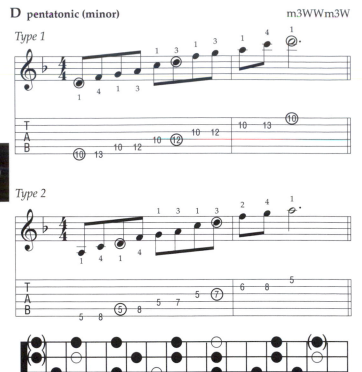

Type 1

Type 2

Dm

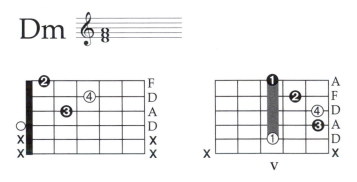

Dm7

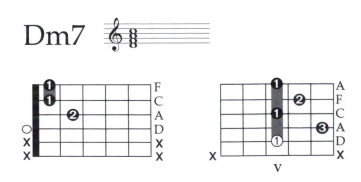

Dm7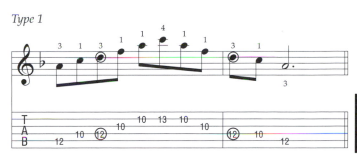

Type 1

D

Type 2

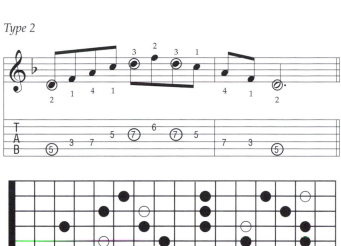

| | V | VII | IX | XII | XV |

D7

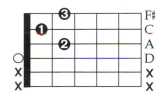

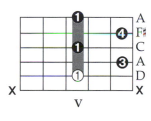

D7#9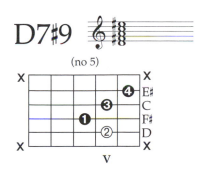

(no 5)

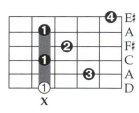

D blues scale (with major third & flatted fifth)   m3HHHHm3W

Type 1

* position shift

Type 2

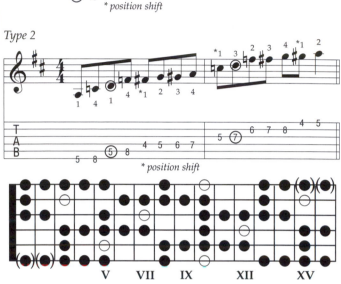

* position shift

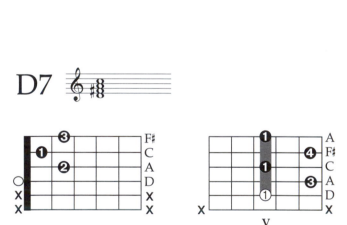

D7

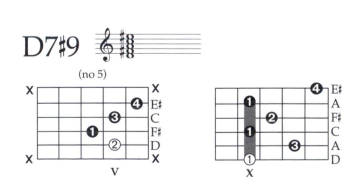

D7♯9
(no 5)

D7♯9

D

Type 1

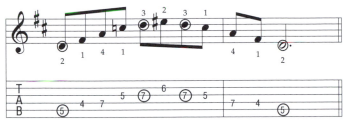

Type 2

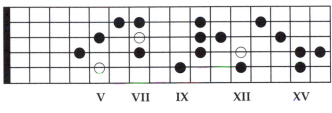

V   VII   IX   XII   XV

D9

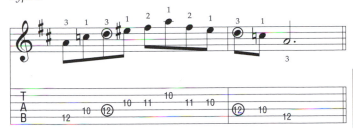

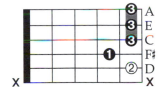

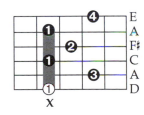

D13

(no 5)   (no 5)

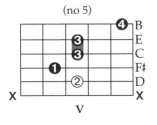

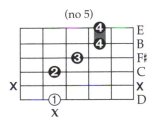

D diminished (whole-half)

WHWHWHWH

Type 1

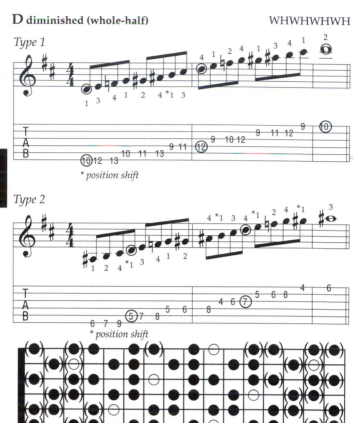

*position shift

Type 2

* position shift

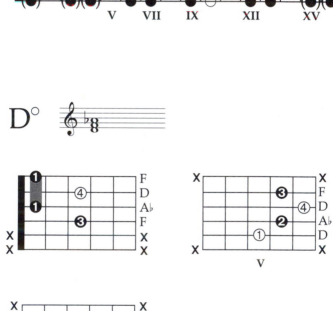

V · VII · IX · XII · XV

D°

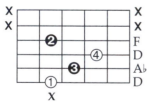

F
D
A♭
F
X
X

X · X
F
D
A♭
D
X

V

X · X
X · X
F
D
A♭
D
X

D°7

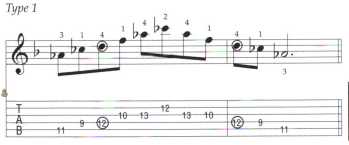

Type 1

Type 2

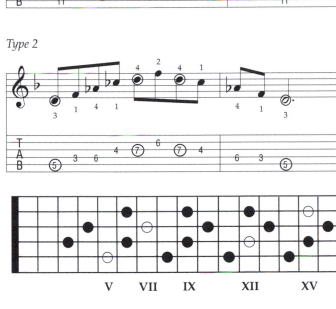

D

D°7

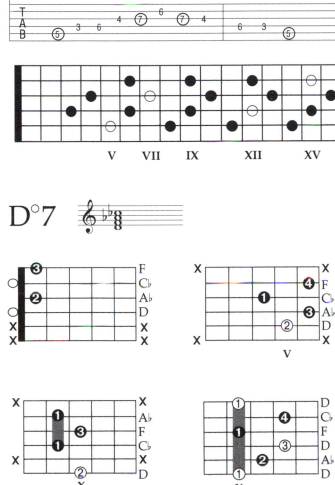

D#/Eb major (Ionian)

WWHWWWH

Type 1

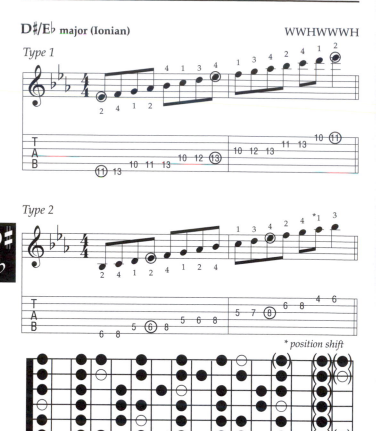

Type 2

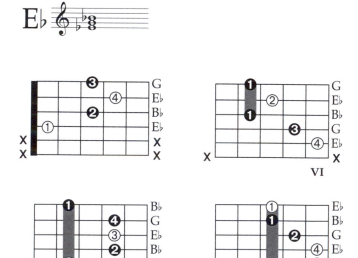

* *position shift*

E♭maj7

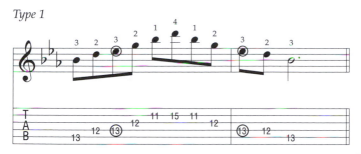

Type 1

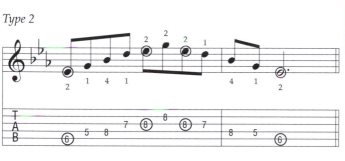

Type 2

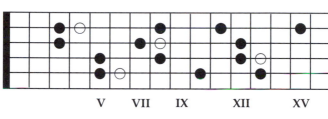

V   VII   IX   XII   XV

E♭maj7

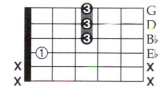

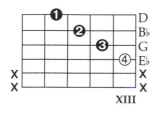

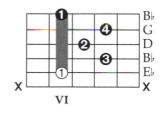

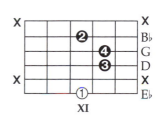

D♯/E♭ natural minor (Aeolian)

WHWWHWW

Type 1

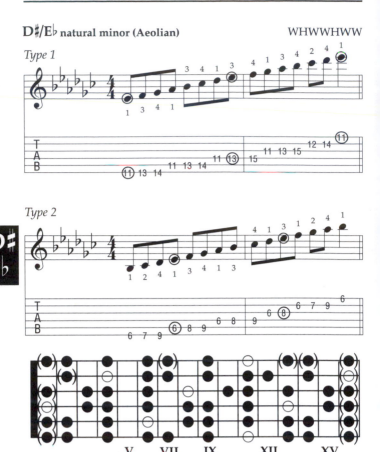

Type 2

E♭m

E♭m7

E♭m

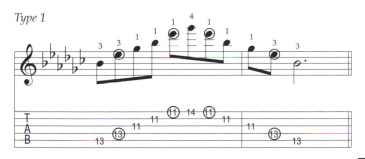

Type 1

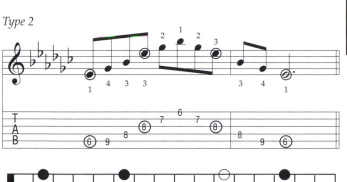

Type 2

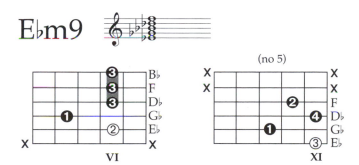

D♯
E♭

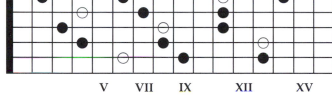

V   VII   IX   XII   XV

E♭m add9

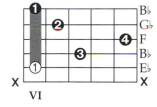

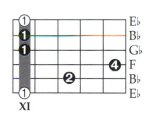

VI

B♭
G♭
F
B♭
E♭

XI

E♭
B♭
G♭
F
B♭
E♭

E♭m9

(no 5)

B♭
F
D♭
G♭
E♭

VI

X
X
F
D♭
G♭
E♭

XI

D♯/E♭ harmonic minor   WHWWHm3H

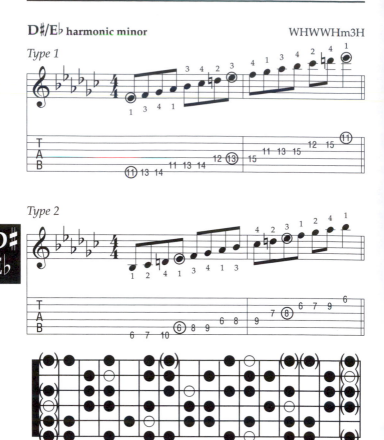

E♭m(maj7)

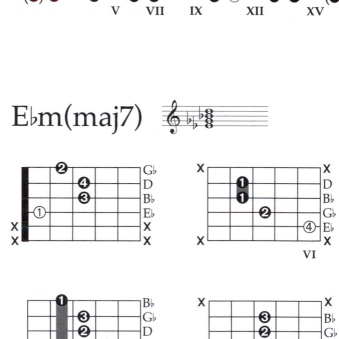

Ebm(maj7)

Type 1

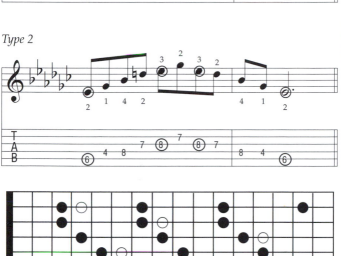

Type 2

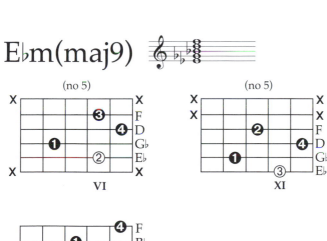

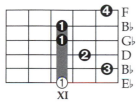

D#
Eb

Ebm(maj9)

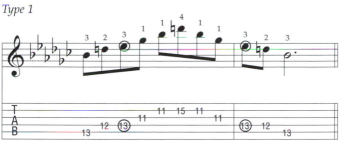

D♯/E♭ jazz minor   WHWWWWH

Type 1

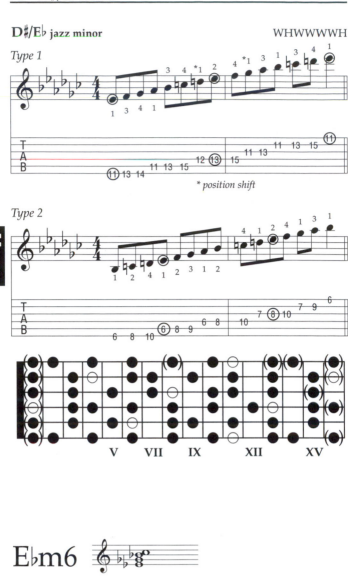

* position shift

Type 2

D♯ E♭

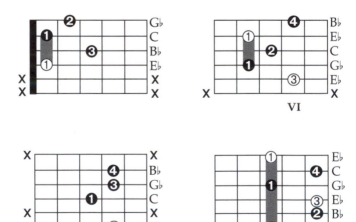

E♭m6

E♭m6

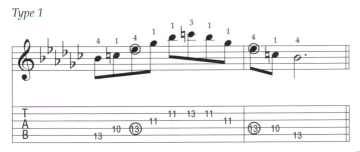

Type 1

Type 2

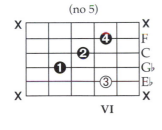

V   VII   IX   XII   XV

E♭m⁶₉

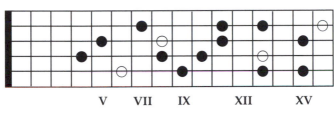

(no 5)

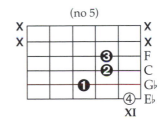

F
C
G♭
E♭

VI

(no 5)

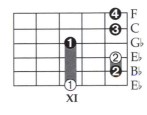

F
C
G♭
E♭

XI

(no 5)

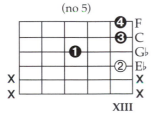

F
C
G♭
E♭

XIII

F
C
G♭
E♭
B♭
E♭

XI

D♯
E♭

D#/Eb Mixolydian

WWHWWHW

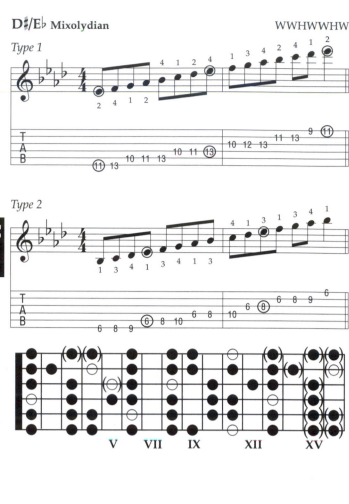

Type 1

Type 2

Eb7

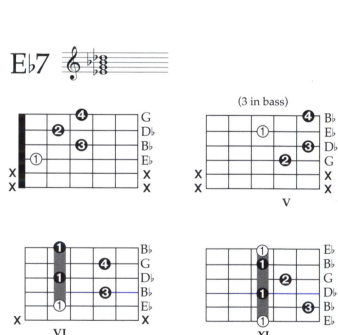

(3 in bass)

E♭7

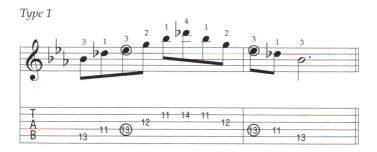

Type 1

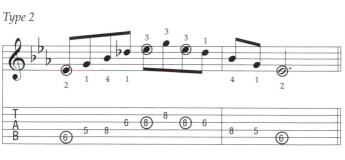

Type 2

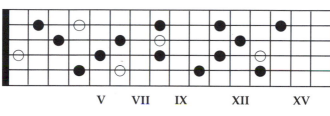

V   VII   IX   XII   XV

E♭9

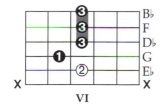

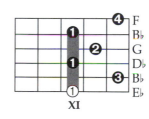

E♭13

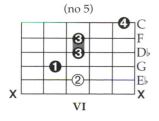

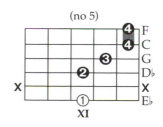

D#
E♭

D♯/E♭ whole tone WWWWWW

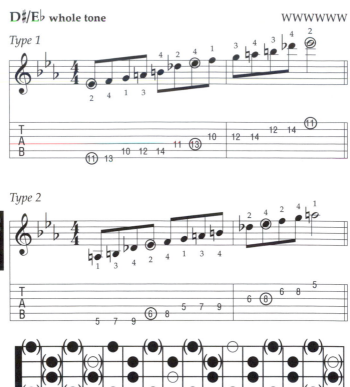

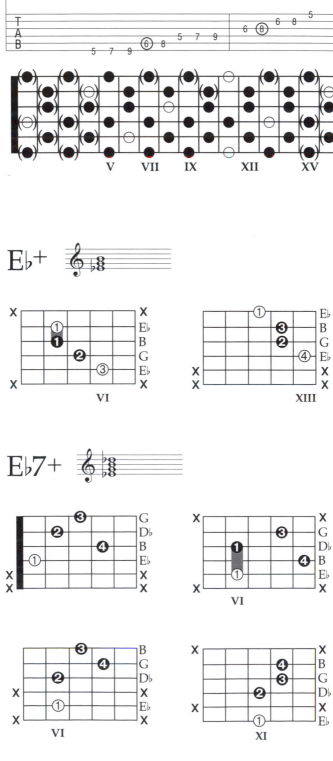

E♭+

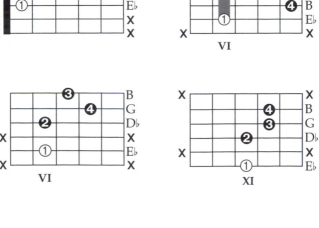

E♭7+

E♭7+

Type 1

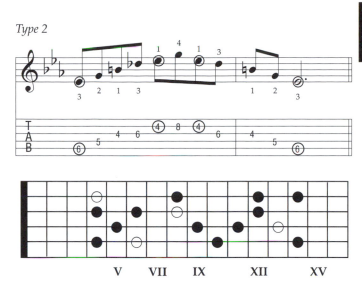

Type 2

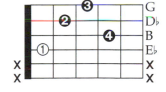

V   VII   IX   XII   XV

E♭7+

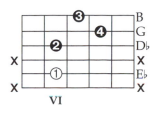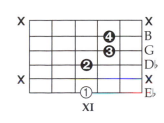

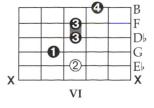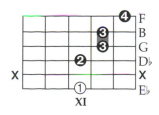

E♭9+

D♯/E♭ pentatonic (major)

WWm3Wm3

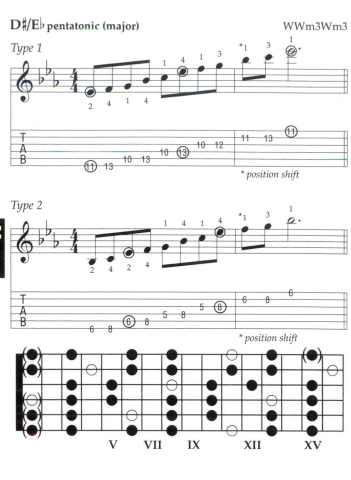

Type 1

position shift

Type 2

position shift

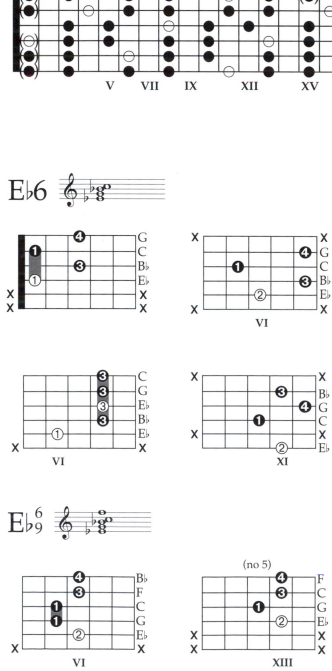

E♭6

E♭$\frac{6}{9}$

(no 5)

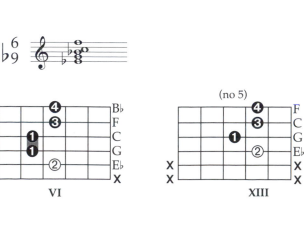

E♭6

Type 1

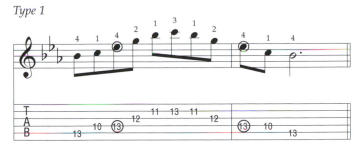

Type 2

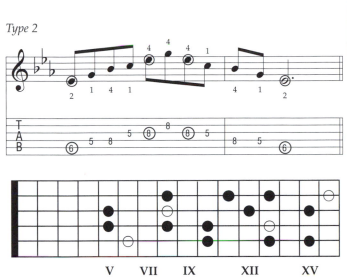

D#
E♭

V   VII   IX   XII   XV

E♭add9

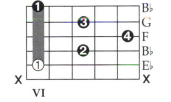

| | B♭ |
| G |
| F |
| B♭ |
| E♭ |

X   X
VI

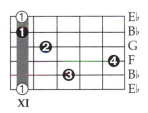

| | E♭ |
| B♭ |
| G |
| F |
| B♭ |
| E♭ |

XI

D♯/E♭ pentatonic (minor)

m3WWm3W

Type 1

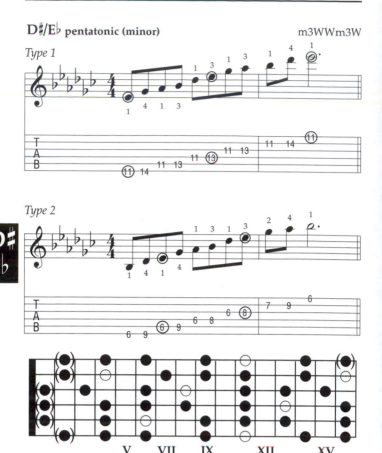

Type 2

E♭m

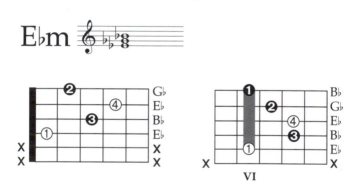

E♭m7

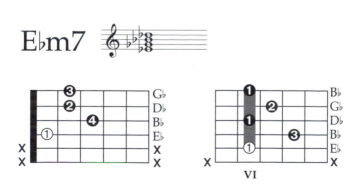

E♭m7

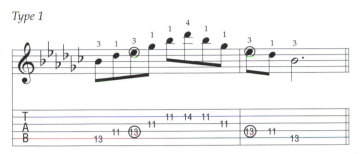

Type 1

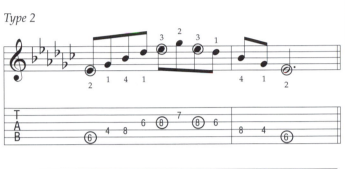

Type 2

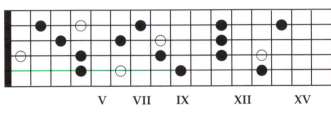

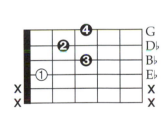

V   VII   IX   XII   XV

E♭7

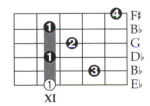

E♭7#9

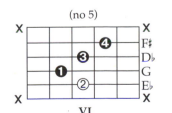

D♯/E♭ blues scale (with major third & flatted fifth) m3HHHHm3W

Type 1

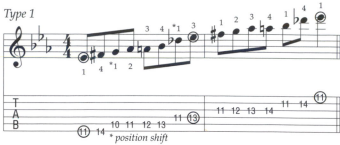

Type 2

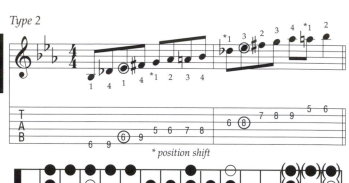

* position shift

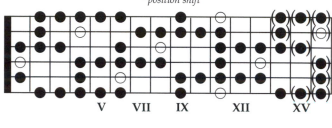

E♭7

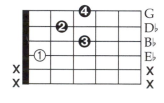

G
D♭
B♭
E♭
X
X

E♭
D♭
G
D♭
B♭
E♭

XI

E♭7♯9

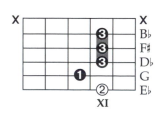

X
B♭
F♯
D♭
G
E♭

XI

(no 5)

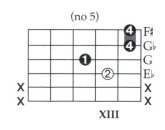

F♯
G♭
G
E♭
X
X

XIII

Eb7#9

Type 1

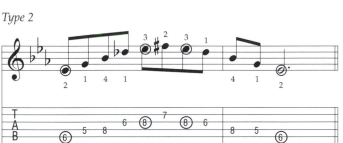

Type 2

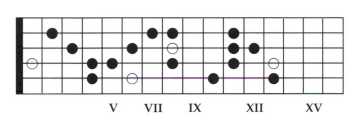

V   VII   IX   XII   XV

Eb9

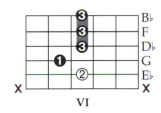 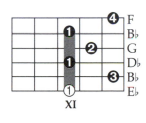

Eb13

(no 5)   (no 5)

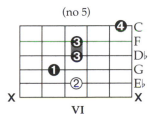 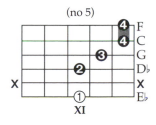

D♯/E♭ diminished (whole-half)

WHWHWHWH

Type 1

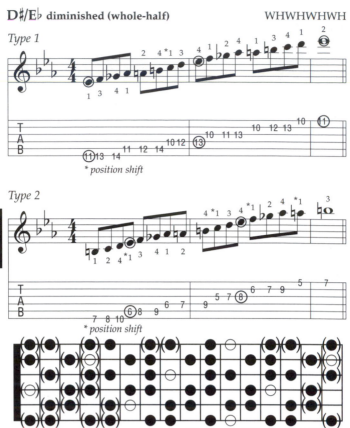

* position shift

Type 2

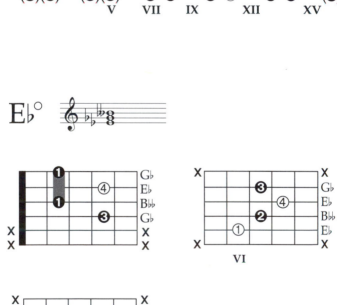

* position shift

E♭°

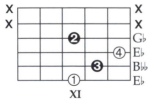

E♭°7

Type 1

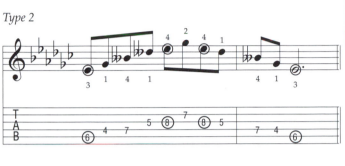

Type 2

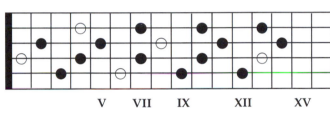

V　　VII　　IX　　XII　　XV

D♯
E♭

E♭°7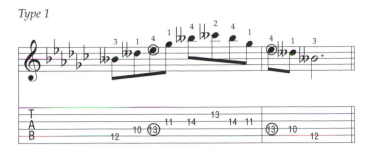

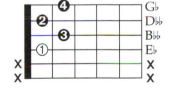

G♭
D♭♭
B♭♭
E♭

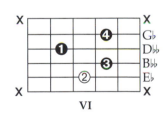

VI

G♭
D♭♭
B♭♭
E♭

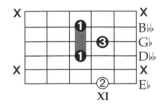

XI

B♭♭
G♭
D♭♭
E♭

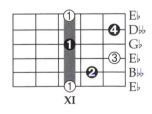

XI

E♭
D♭♭
G♭
E♭
B♭♭
E♭

E major (Ionian)

WWHWWWH

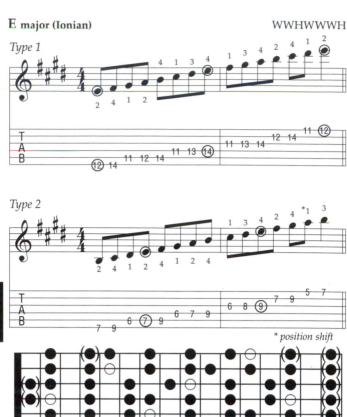

Type 1

Type 2

* position shift

V VII IX XII XV

E

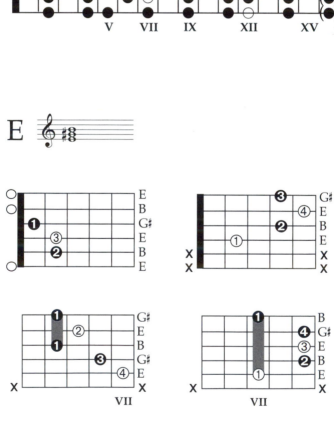

VII

VII

Emaj7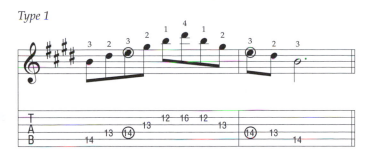

Type 1

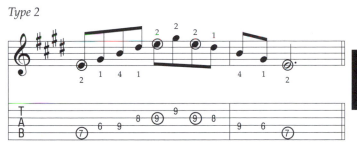

Type 2

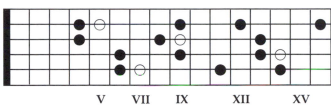

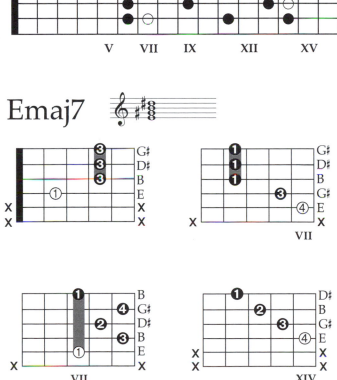

V   VII   IX   XII   XV

E

Emaj7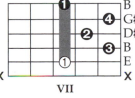

E natural minor (Aeolian)

WHWWHWW

Type 1

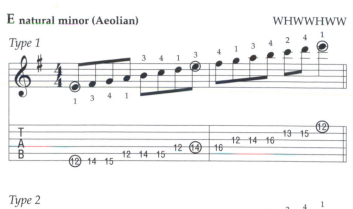

Type 2

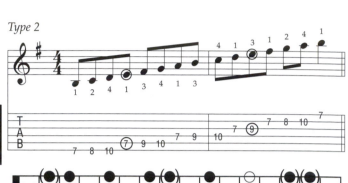

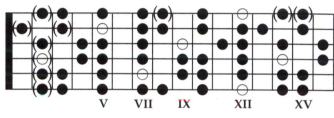

V   VII   IX   XII   XV

Em

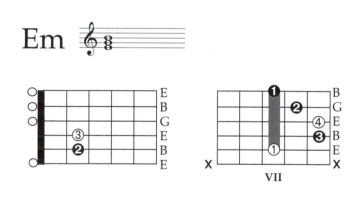

Em7

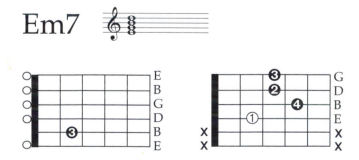

Em

Type 1

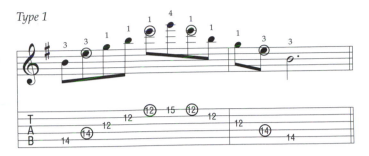

Type 2

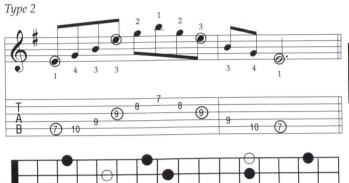

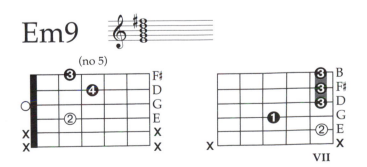

V   VII   IX   XII   XV

Em add9

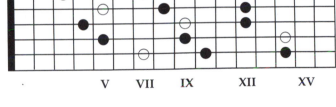

E
B
G
F♯
B
E

B
G
F♯
B
E

VII

Em9

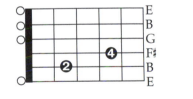

(no 5)

F♯
D
G
E
X
X

B
F♯
D
G
E
X

VII

E

E harmonic minor

WHWWHm3H

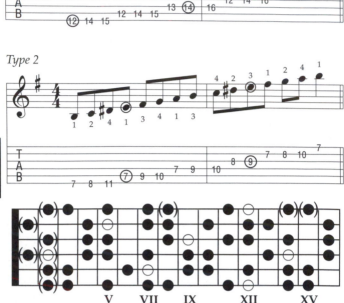

Type 1

Type 2

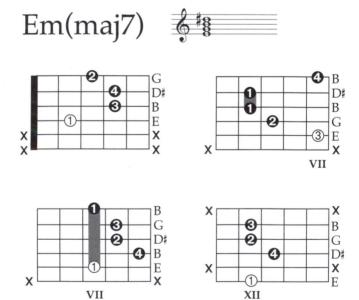

V   VII   IX   XII   XV

Em(maj7)

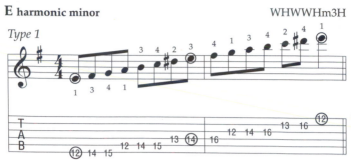

Em(maj7)

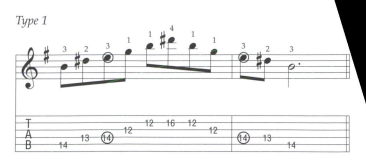

Type 1

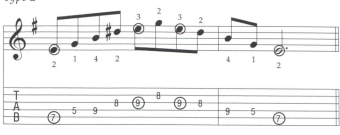

Type 2

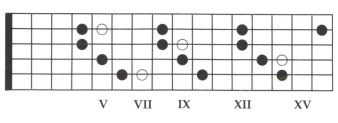

| V | VII | IX | XII | XV |

E

Em(maj9)

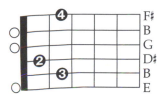

(no 5)

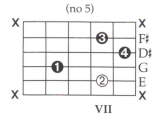

VII

(no 5)

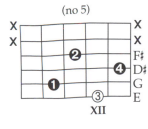

XII

minor

WHWWWWH

* position shift

Type 2

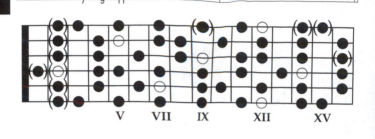

V   VII   IX   XII   XV

Em6

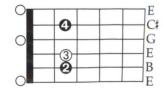

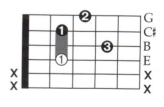

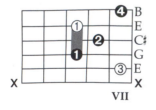

VII

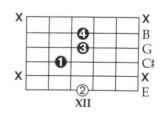

XII

Em6

Type 1

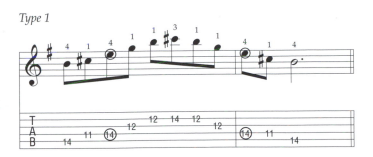

Type 2

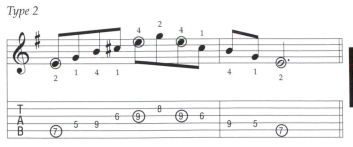

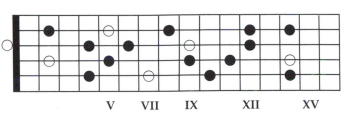

| | V | VII | IX | XII | XV |

Em 6/9

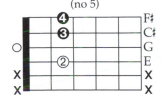

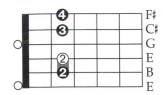

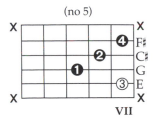

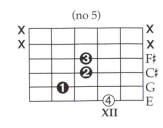

E

Mixolydian   WWHWWHW

Type 1

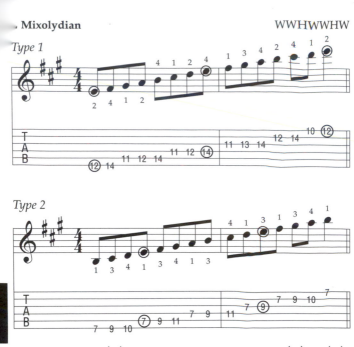

Type 2

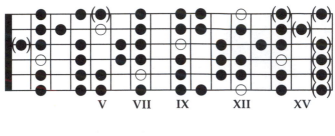

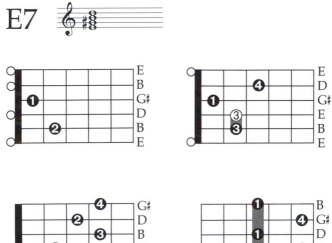

V   VII   IX   XII   XV

E7

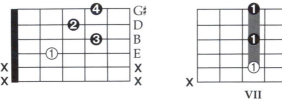

E
B
G#
D
B
E

E
D
G#
E
B
E

G#
D
B
E
X
X

B
G#
D
B
E
X

VII

E7

Type 1

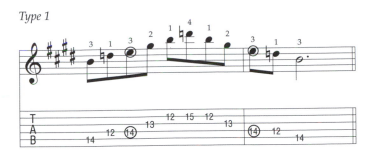

Type 2

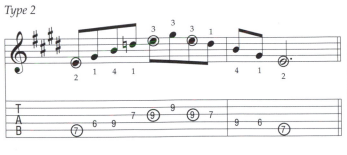

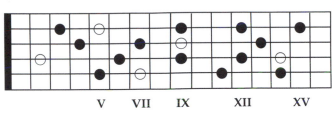

V   VII   IX   XII   XV

E

E9

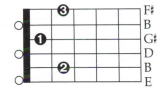

F#
B
G#
D
B
E

(no 5)

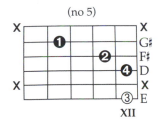

X   X
G#
F#
D
X
E
XII

E13

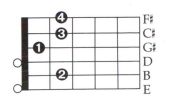

F#
C#
G#
D
B
E

(no 5)

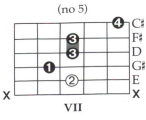

C#
F#
D
G#
E
VII

E whole tone

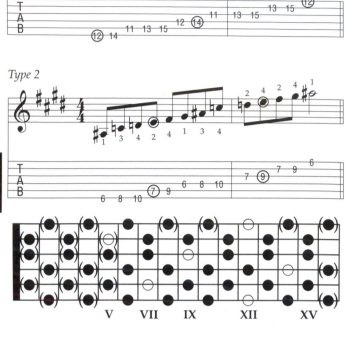

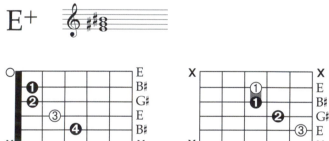

E+

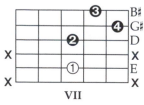

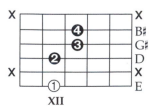

E7+

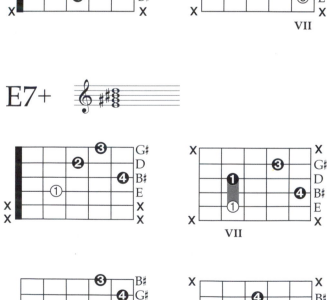

E

E7+

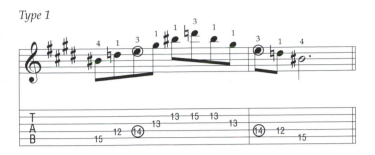

Type 1

Type 2

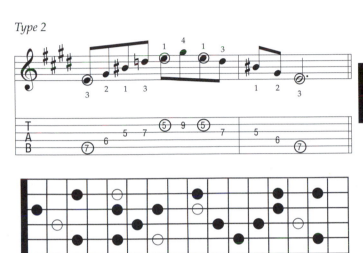

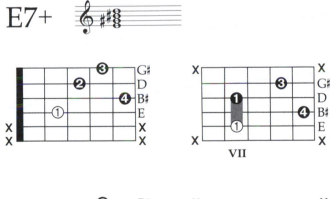

E

E7+

E9+

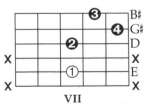
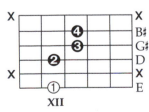

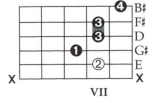
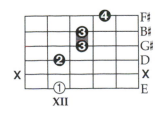

E pentatonic (major)

WWm3Wm3

Type 1

* position shift

Type 2

* position shift

V   VII   IX   XII   XV

E6

E
C#
G#
E
B
E

G#
C#
B
E
X
X

X   X
                     G#
                     C#
                     B
                     E
X   X

VII

X   X
                     B
                     G#
                     C#
                     X
X   E

XII

E $^6_9$

(no 5)

F#
C#
G#
E
X
X

B
F#
C#
G#
E
X

VII

E6

Type 1

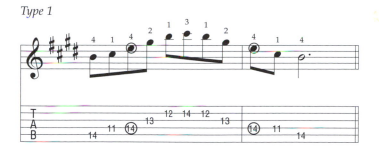

Type 2

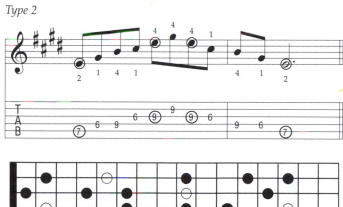

E

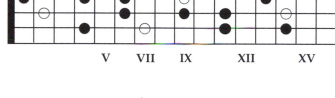

V   VII   IX   XII   XV

Eadd9

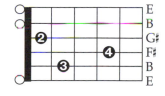

E pentatonic (minor)

m3WWm3W

Type 1

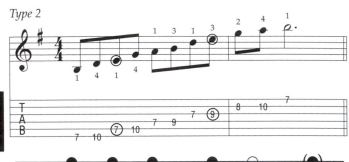

Type 2

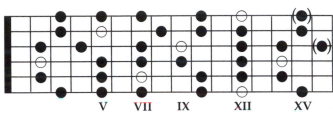

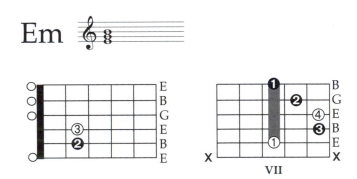

V   VII   IX   XII   XV

Em

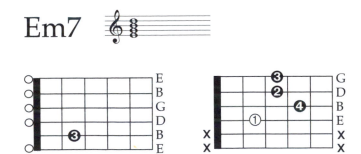

Em7

Type 1

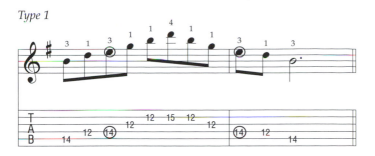

Type 2

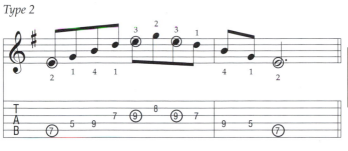

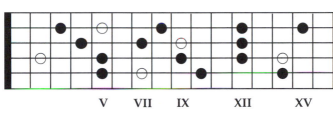

V VII IX XII XV

E7

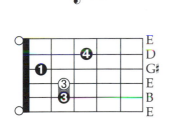

E D G# E B E

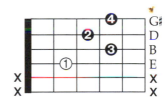

G# D B E X X

E7♯9

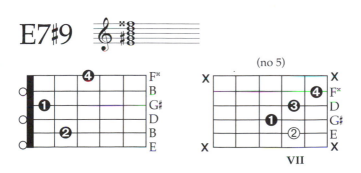

(no 5)

F* B G# D B E

F* D G# E

VII

E

E blues scale (with major third & flatted fifth)

m3HHHHm3W

Type 1

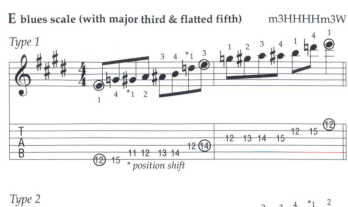

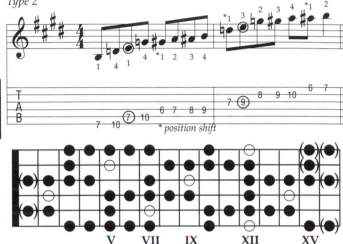

Type 2

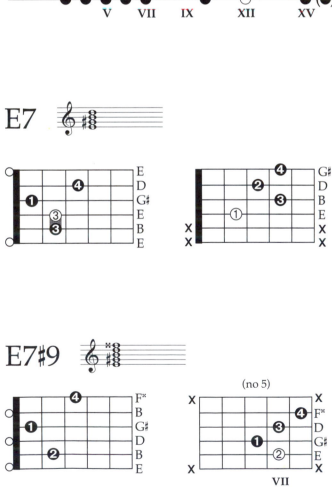

E7

E7#9

(no 5)

E7#9

Type 1

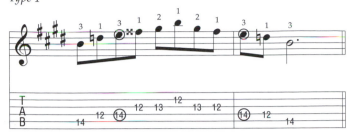

Type 2

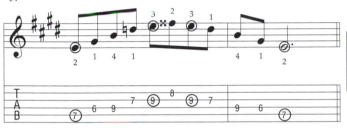

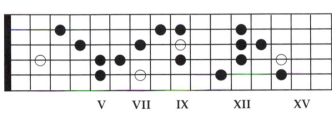

E

E9

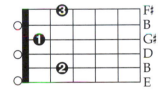 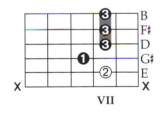

E13

(no 5)

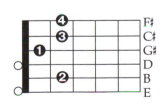 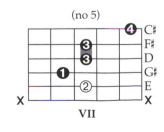

E diminished (whole-half)

WHWHWHWH

Type 1

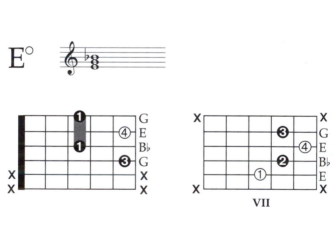

* position shift

Type 2

* position shift

V   VII   IX   XII   XV

E°

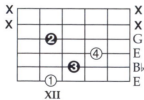

E°7

Type 1

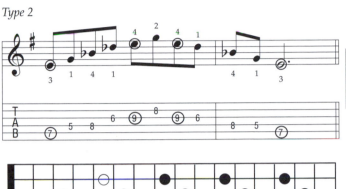

Type 2

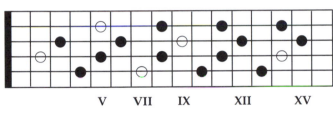

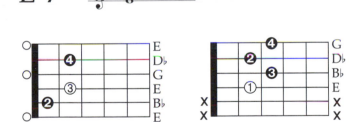

V   VII   IX   XII   XV

E

E°7

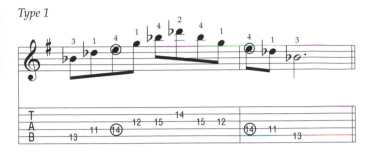

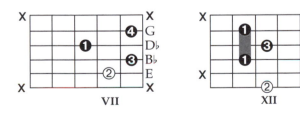

VII   XII

F major (Ionian)

WWHWWWH

Type 1

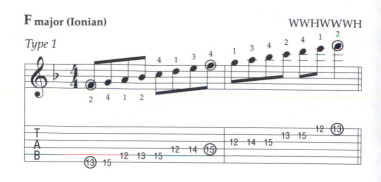

Type 2

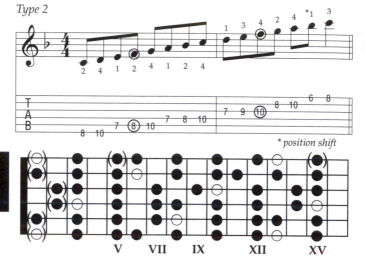

* position shift

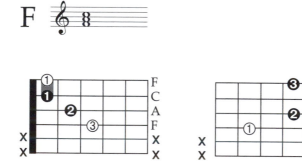

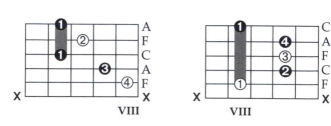

Fmaj7

Type 1

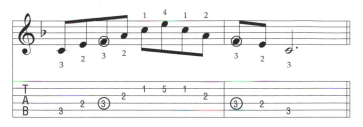

Type 2

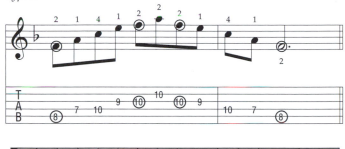

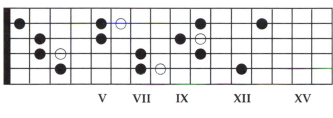

V   VII   IX   XII   XV

F

Fmaj7

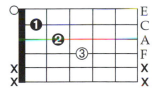

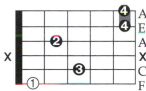

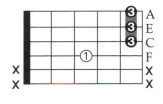

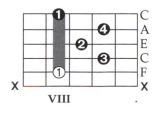

F natural minor (Aeolian)   WHWWHWW

Type 1

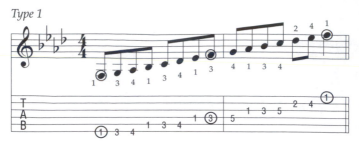

Type 2

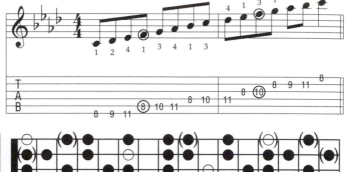

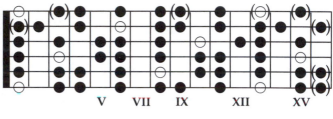

V   VII   IX   XII   XV

Fm

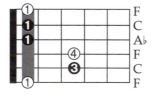

F
C
A♭
F
C
F

A♭
F
C
F
X
X

III

Fm7

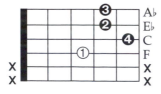

A♭
E♭
C
F
X
X

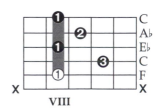

C
A♭
E♭
C
F
X

VIII

Fm

Type 1

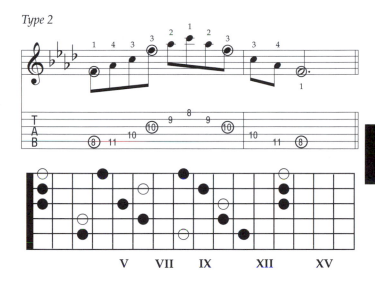

Type 2

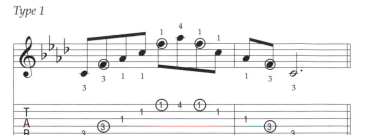

F

Fm add9

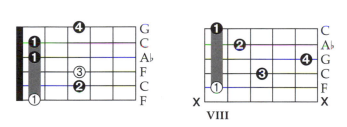

Fm9

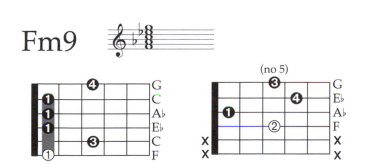

F harmonic minor WHWWHm3H

Type 1

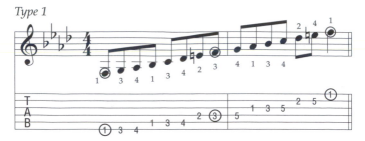

Type 2

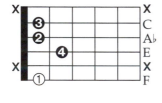
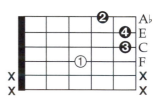

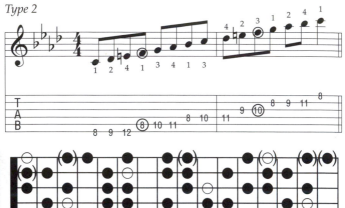

V   VII   IX   XII   XV

Fm(maj7)

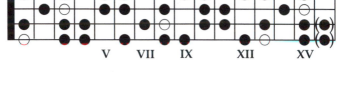

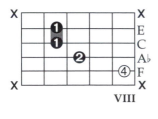
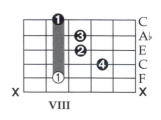

Fm(maj7)

Type 1

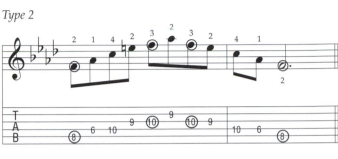

Type 2

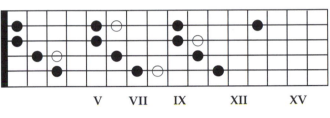

V   VII   IX   XII   XV

F

Fm(maj9)

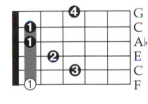

(no 5)

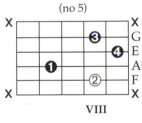

VIII

(no 5)

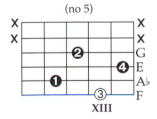

XIII

F jazz minor   WHWWWWH

Type 1

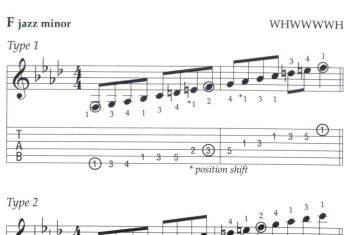

* position shift

Type 2

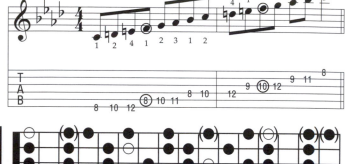

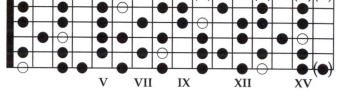

Fm6

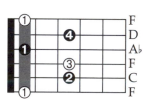

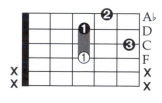

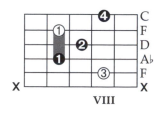

VIII

Fm6

Type 1

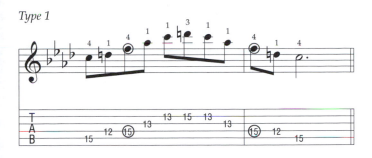

Type 2

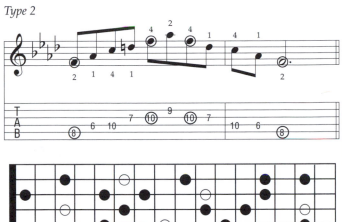

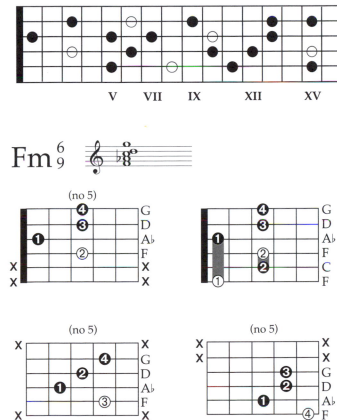

V VII IX XII XV

Fm $^6_9$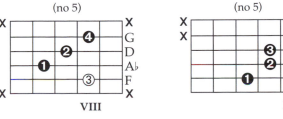

F

F Mixolydian

WWHWWHW

Type 1

Type 2

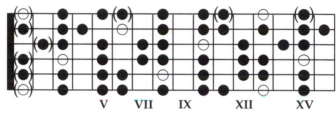

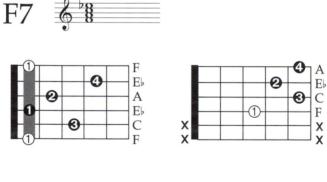

| V | VII | IX | XII | XV |

F7

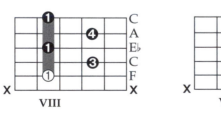

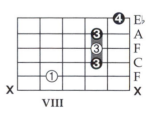

F7

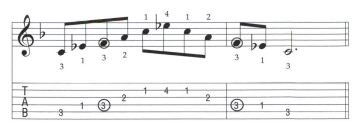

Type 1

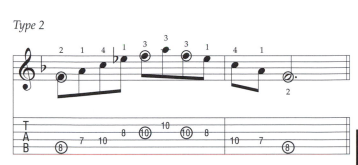

Type 2

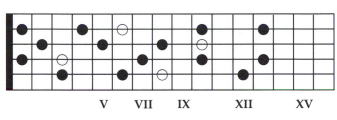

V   VII   IX   XII   XV

F

F9

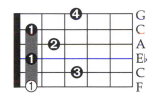

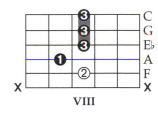

F13

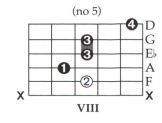

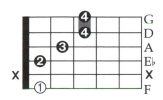

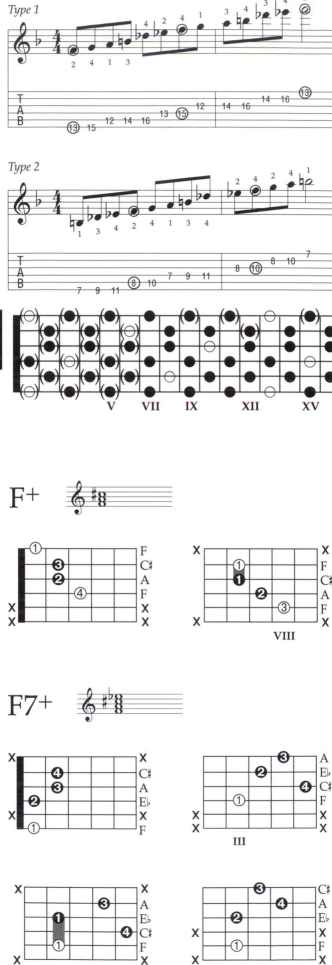

F7+

Type 1

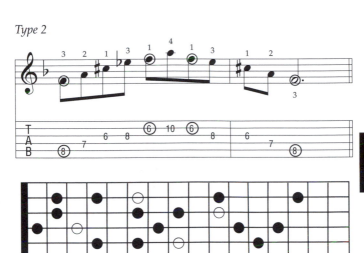

Type 2

F

F7+

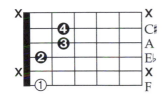

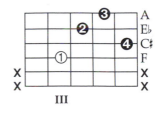

F9+

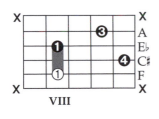

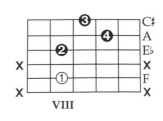

F pentatonic (major)

WWm3Wm3

Type 1

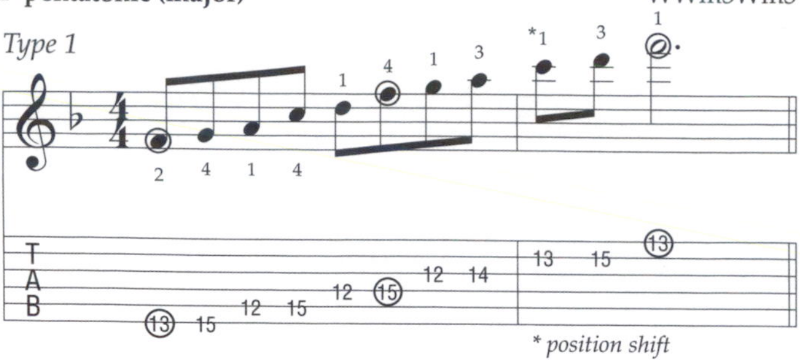

* position shift

Type 2

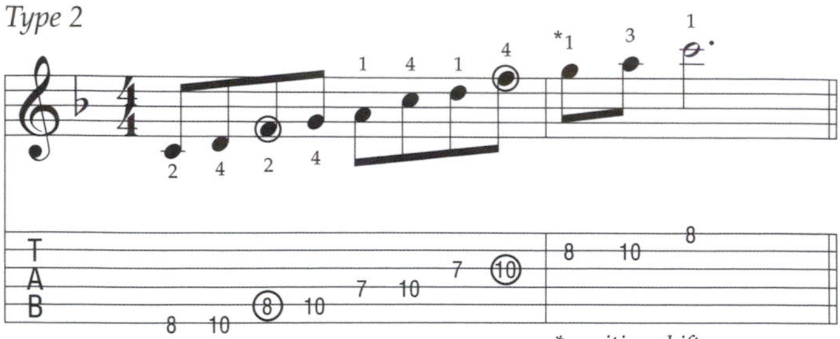

* position shift

V   VII   IX   XII   XV

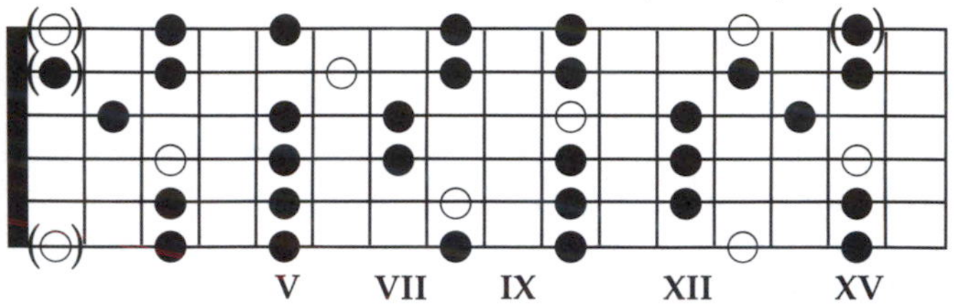

F6

(no 5)

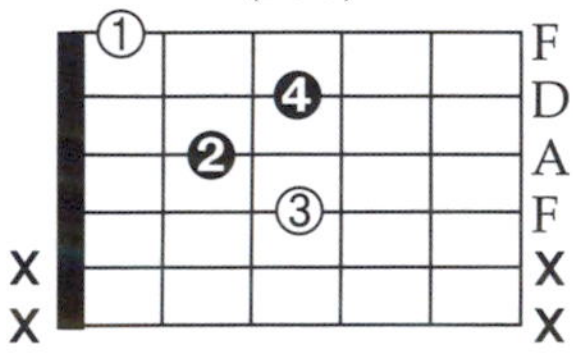

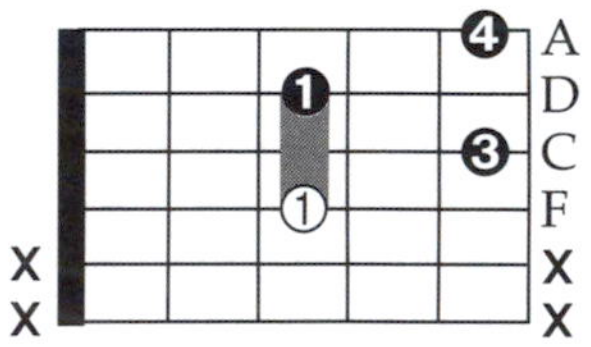

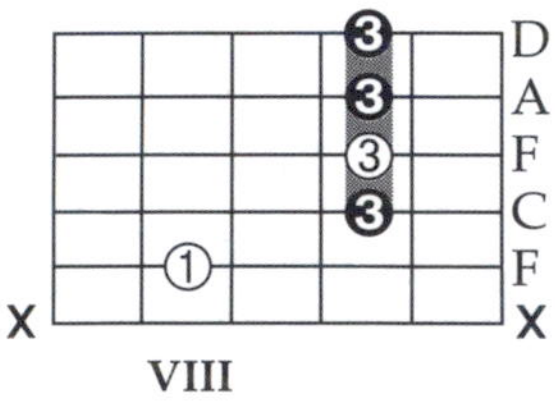

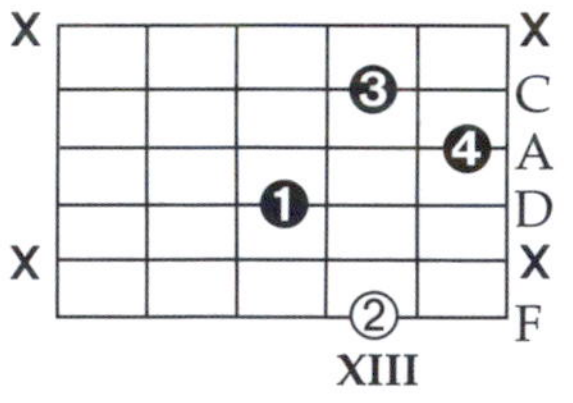

F⁶₉

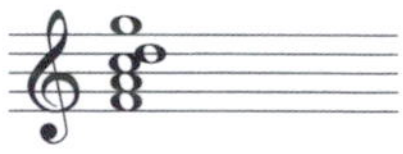

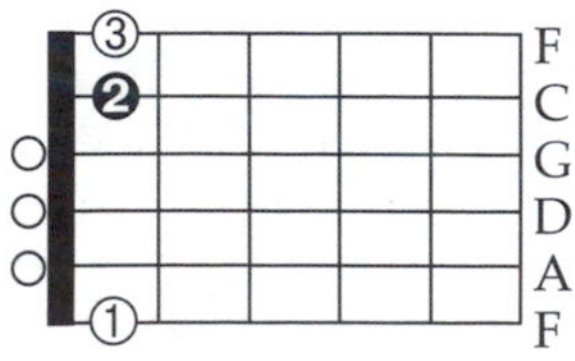

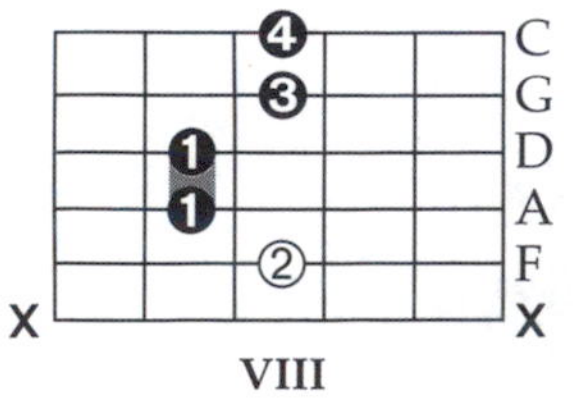

F6

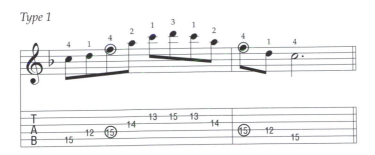

Type 1

Type 2

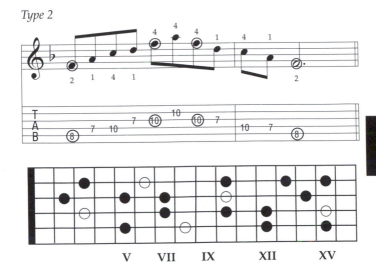

V   VII   IX   XII   XV

F

Fadd9

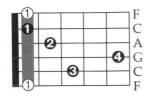

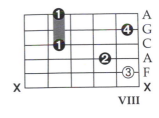

F pentatonic (minor)

m3WWm3W

Type 1

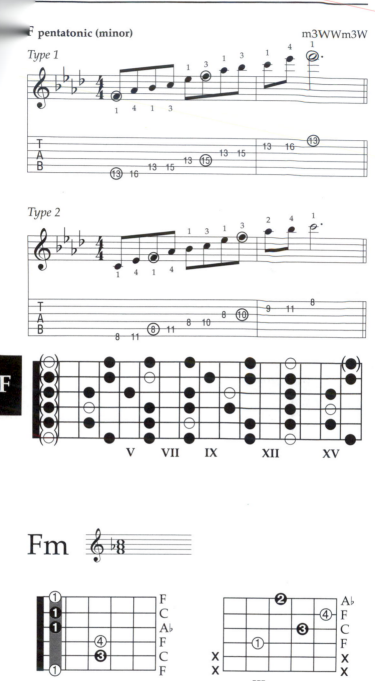

Type 2

V   VII   IX   XII   XV

F

Fm

Fm7

Fm7

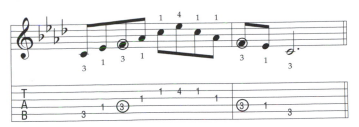

Type 1

Type 2

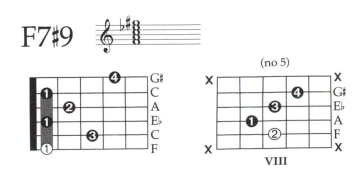

V   VII   IX   XII   XV

F7

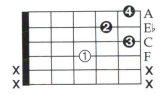

F7♯9

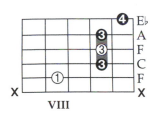

F blues scale (with major third & flatted fifth)

m3HHHHm3W

Type 1

position shift

Type 2

position shift

| | V | VII | IX | XII | XV |

F7

F
C
A
Eb
C
F

C
A
Eb
C
F

VIII

F7#9

G#
C
A
Eb
C
F

(no 5)

G#
Eb
A
F

F7#9

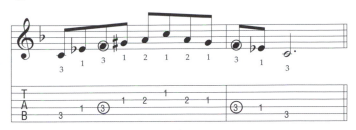

Type 1

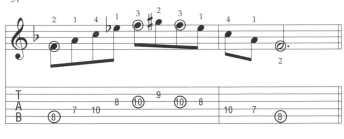

Type 2

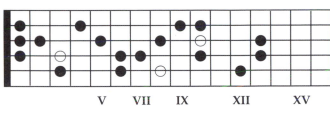

V   VII   IX   XII   XV

F

F9

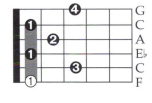

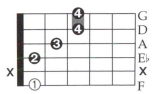

G
C
A
Eb
C
F

VIII

C
G
Eb
A
F

F13

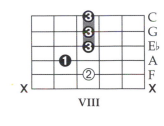

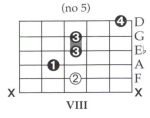

(no 5)

G
D
A
Eb
F

VIII

D
G
Eb
A
F

F diminished (whole-half)

WHWHWHWH

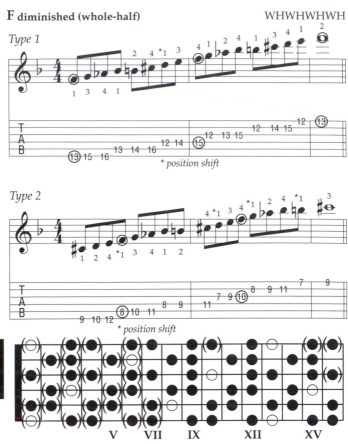

Type 1

* position shift

Type 2

* position shift

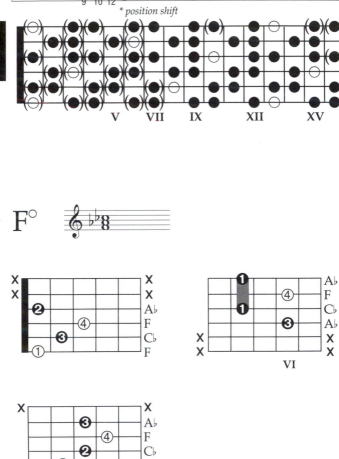

V   VII   IX   XII   XV

F°

F°7

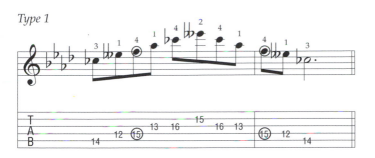

Type 1

Type 2

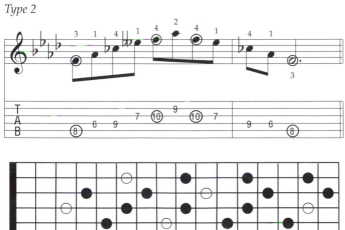

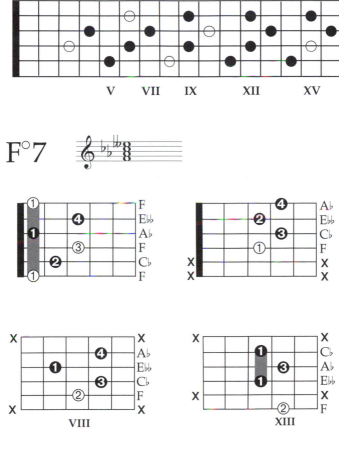

F

F°7

F#/G♭ major (Ionian)

WWHWWWH

Type 1

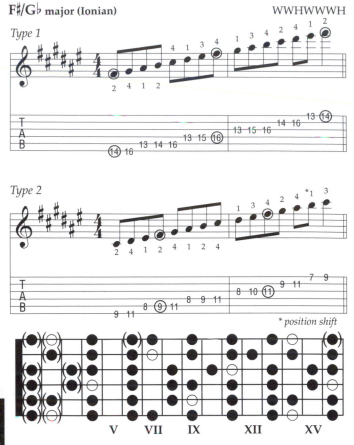

Type 2

* position shift

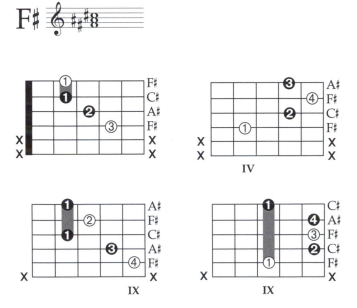

F#maj7

Type 1

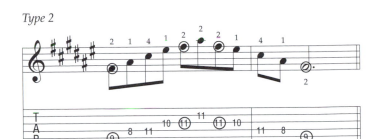

Type 2

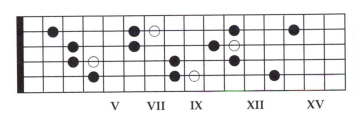

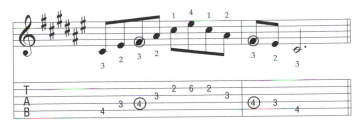

V   VII   IX   XII   XV

F#maj7

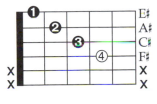

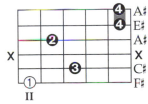

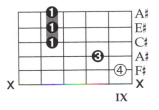

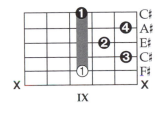

F♯/G♭ natural minor (Aeolian)

WHWWHWW

Type 1

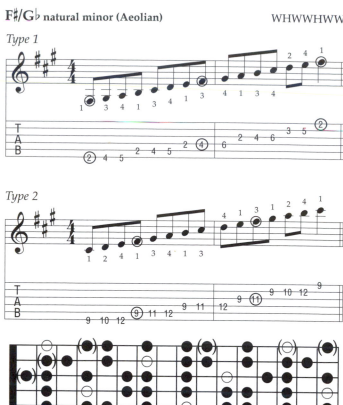

Type 2

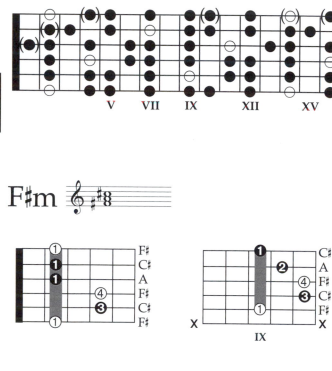

F♯m

F♯m7

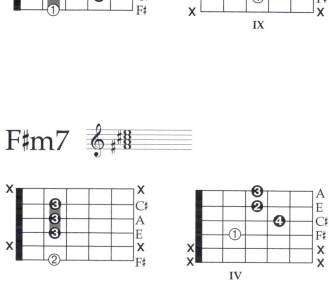

F♯m

Type 1

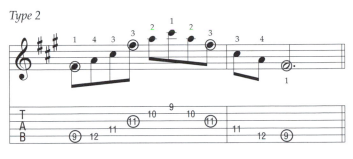

Type 2

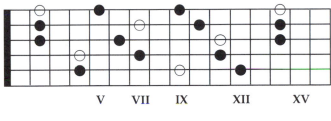

F♯m add9

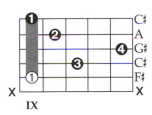

F♯m9

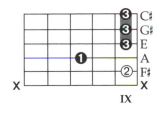

F#/G♭ harmonic minor   WHWWHm3H

Type 1

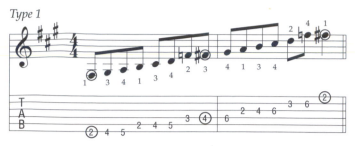

Type 2

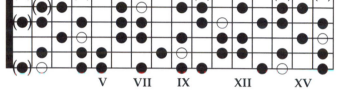

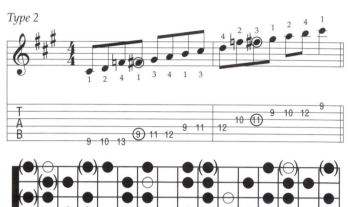

V   VII   IX   XII   XV

F#m(maj7)

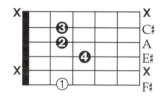

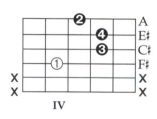

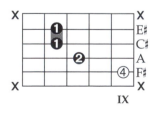

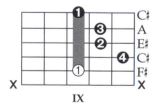

F#m(maj7)

Type 1

Type 2

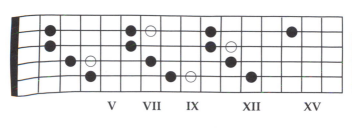

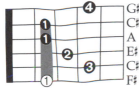

F#
Gb

F#m(maj9)

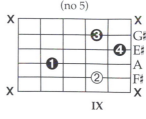

(no 5)

IX

(no 5)

XIV

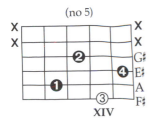

jazz minor

WHWWWWH

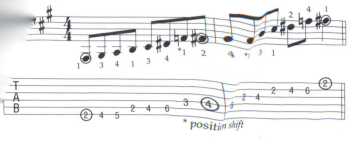

Type 2

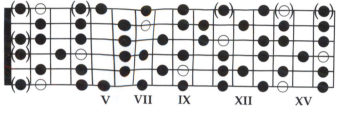

* *position shift*

V   VII   IX   XII   XV

F#m6

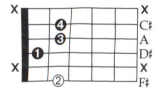

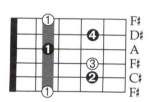

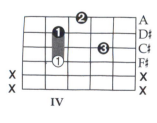

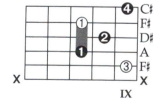

F#m6

Type 1

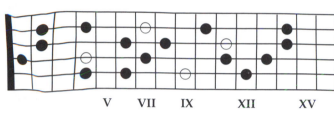

Type 2

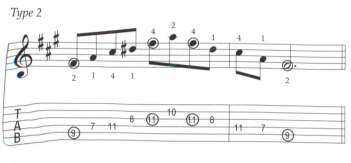

V   VII   IX   XII   XV

F#
Gb

F#m⁶₉

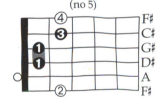

(no 5)

F#
C#
G#
D#
A
F#

(no 5)

G#
D#
A
F#
X
X

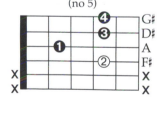

G#
D#
A
F#
C#
F#

(no 5)

X

G#
D#
A
F#
X

IX

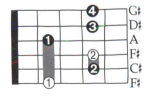

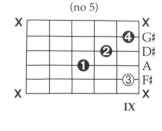

...ydian   WWHWWHW

Type 2

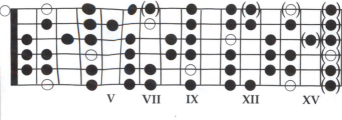

F♯ / G♭

V   VII   IX   XII   XV

F♯7

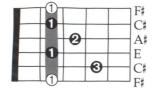

F♯
C♯
A♯
E
C♯
F♯

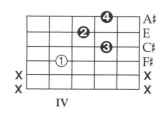

A♯
E
C♯
F♯
X
X

IV

(3 in bass)

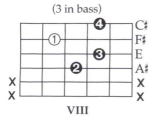

C♯
F♯
E
A♯
X
X

VIII

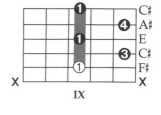

C♯
A♯
E
C♯
F♯
X

IX

Type 2

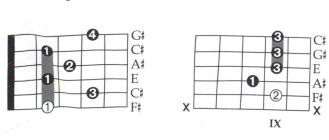

F#9

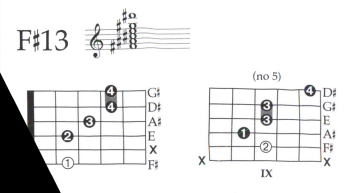

F#13

F#
Gb

F#+

F#7+

IX

IV

IX   IX

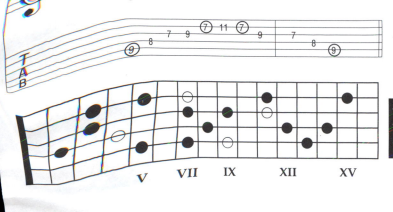

F#7⁺

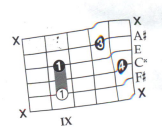

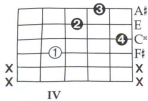

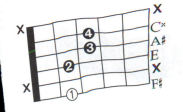

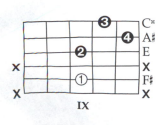

F#9⁺

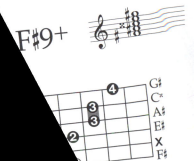

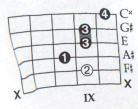

F#6

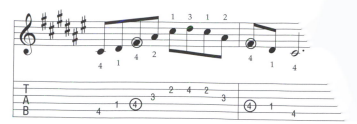

Type 1

Type 2

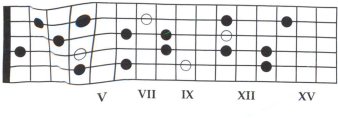

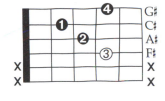

V VII IX XII XV

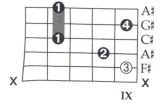

F#add9

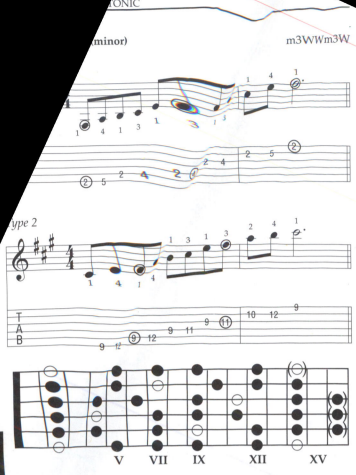

Type 2

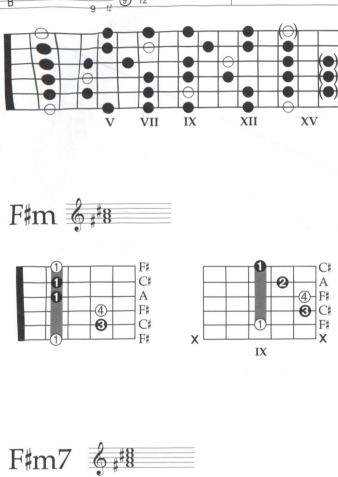

F♯
G♭

F♯m

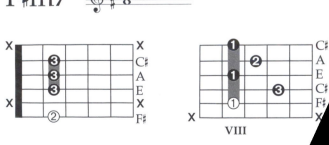

F♯m7

F#m7

Type 1

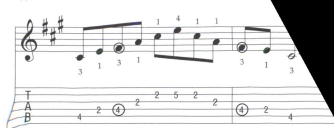

Type 2

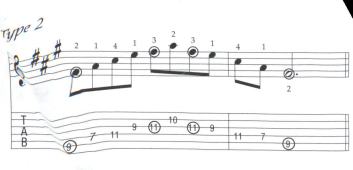

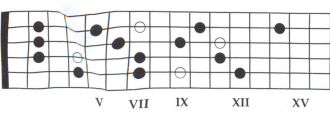

V   VII   IX   XII   XV

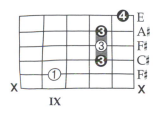

F#7

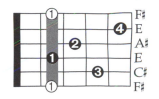

F#7#9

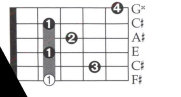

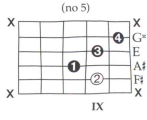

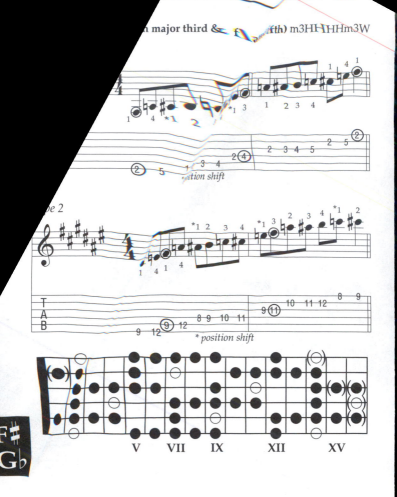

* position shift

* position shift

F#
Gb

V   VII   IX   XII   XV

F#7

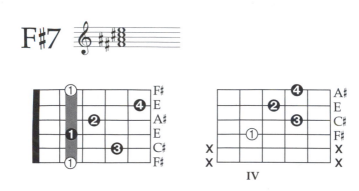

F#
E
A#
E
C#
F#

A#
E
C#
F#
X
X

IV

F#7#9

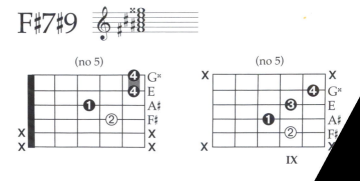

(no 5)

G×
E
A#
F#
X
X

(no 5)

X

G×
E
A#
F#
X

IX

F#7#9

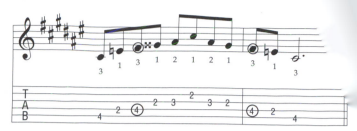

Type 1

Type 2

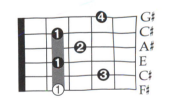

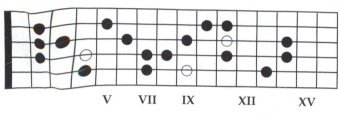

V   VII   IX   XII   XV

F#
Gb

F#9

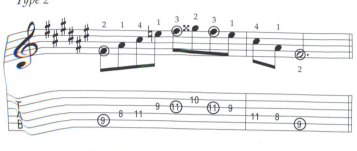

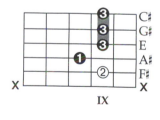

G#
C#
A#
E
C#
F#

C#
G#
E
A#
F#

X   IX   X

F#13

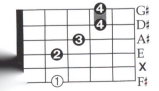

(no 5)

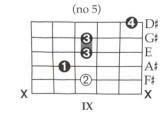

G#
D#
A#
E
X
F#

D#
G#
E
A#
F#

X   IX   X

...shed (whole-half)   **WHWHWHWH**

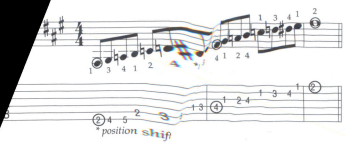

position shift

Type 2

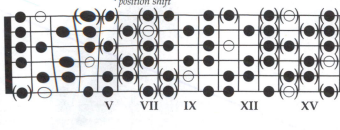

position shift

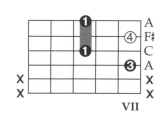

F#
Gb

V   VII   IX   XII   XV

F#°

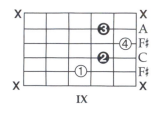

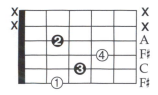

VII

IX

F#°7

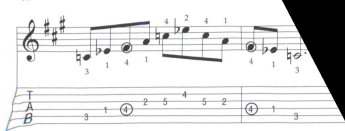

Type 1

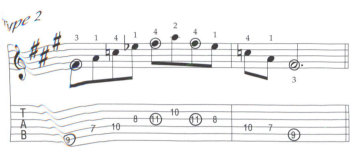

Type 2

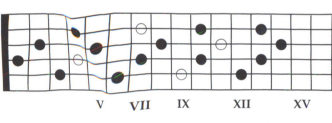

V   VII   IX   XII   XV

F#°7

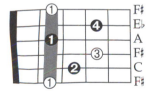

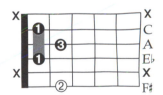

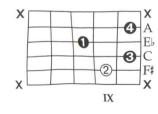

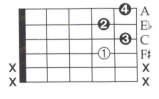

ype 2

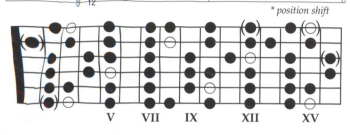

* position shift

V   VII   IX   XII   XV

G

G 𝄞 𝄾

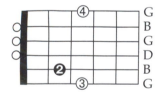

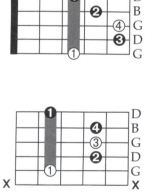

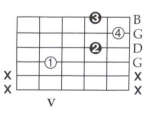

Gmaj7

Type 1

Type 2

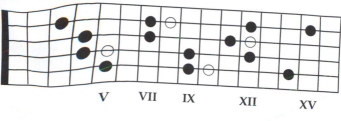

V VII IX XII XV

Gmaj7

F#
B
G
D
X
X

X
X
D
B
F#
X
G

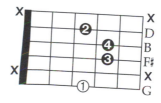
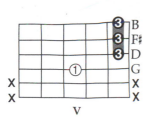
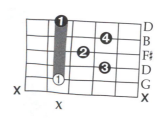

B
F#
D
G
X
X

V

D
B
F#
D
G
X

X

(Aeolian)

WHWWHWW

Type 2

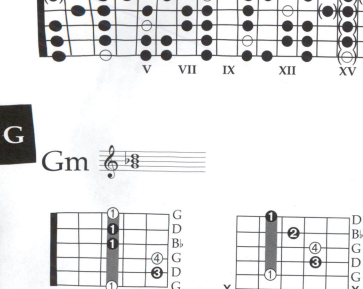

V   VII   IX   XII   XV

G

Gm

G
D
B♭
G
D
G

X   X

D
B♭
G
D
G
X

Gm7

G
D
B♭
F
D
G

B♭
F
D
G
X
X

X
X   V

Gm

Type 1

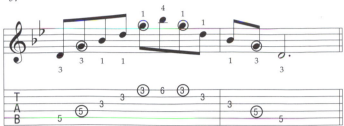

Type 2

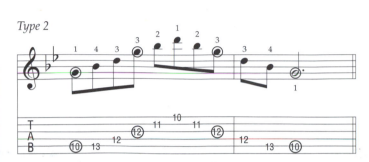

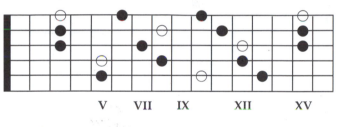

V VII IX XII XV

Gm add9

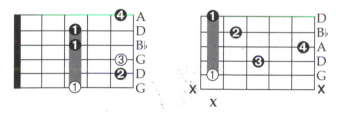

Gm9

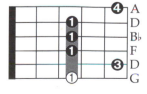
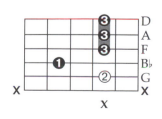

G harmonic minor

WHWWHm3H

Type 1

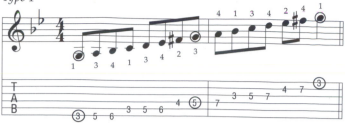

Type 2

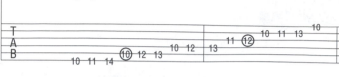

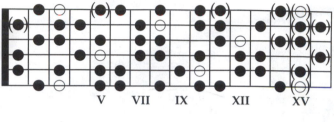

V   VII   IX   XII   XV

G

Gm(maj7)

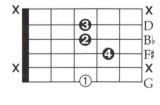

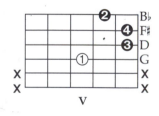

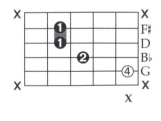

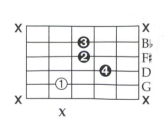

Gm(maj7)

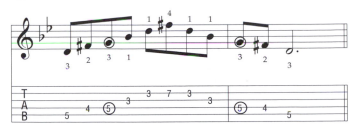

Type 1

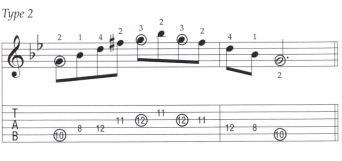

Type 2

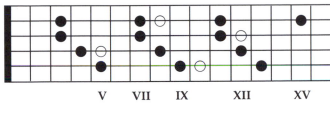

V   VII   IX   XII   XV

G

Gm(maj9)

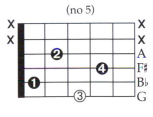

(no 5)

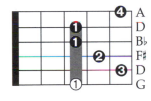

(no 5)

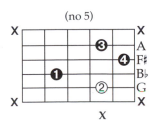

G jazz minor   WHWWWWH

Type 1

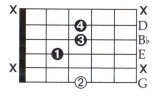

* position shift

Type 2

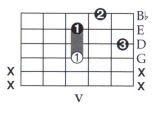

V   VII   IX   XII   XV

G

Gm6

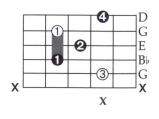

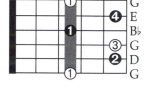

Gm6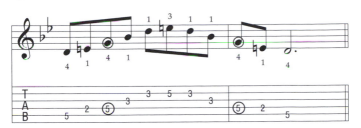

Type 1

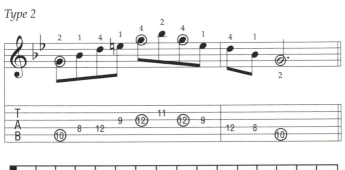

Type 2

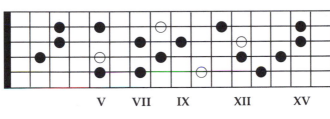

V   VII   IX   XII   XV

G

Gm$_9^6$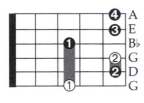

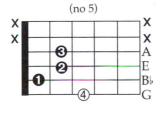

(no 5)

X
X
X — A
③ —
② — E
① — B♭
④ — G

(no 5)

④ — A
❸ — E
❶ — B♭
② — G
X
X

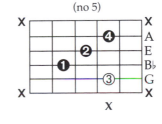

④ — A
❸ — E
❶ — B♭
② — G
❷ — D
① — G

(no 5)

X   X
④ — A
② — E
① — B♭
③ — G
X   X
X

G Mixolydian

WWHWWHW

Type 1

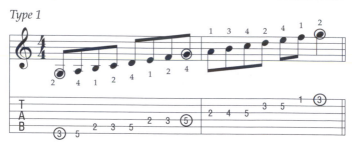

Type 2

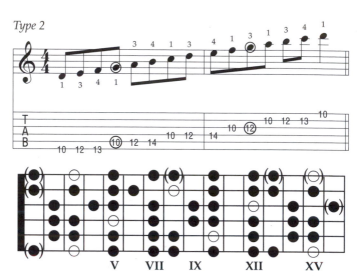

V   VII   IX   XII   XV

G

G7

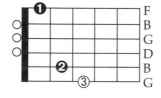

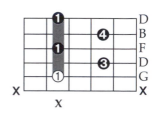

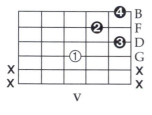

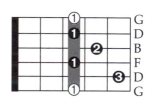

G7

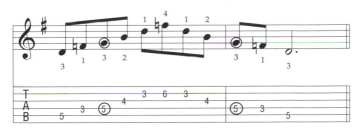

Type 1

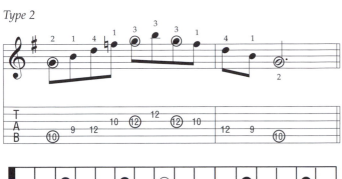

Type 2

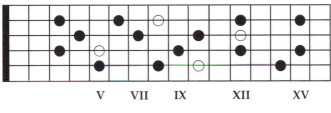

V   VII   IX   XII   XV

G

G9

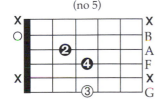

G13

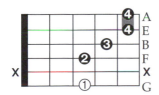

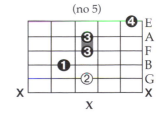

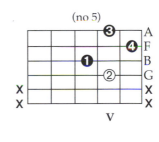

G whole tone

Type 1

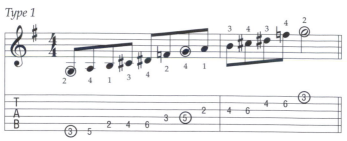

Type 2

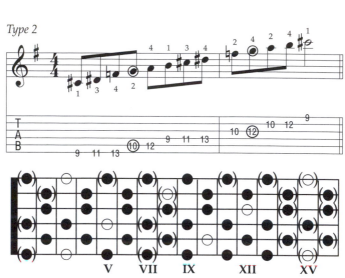

G+

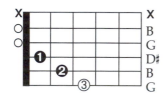
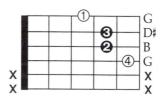

G7+

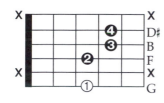
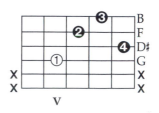

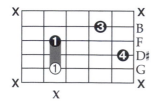
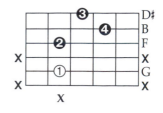

G7+

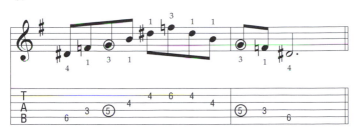

Type 1

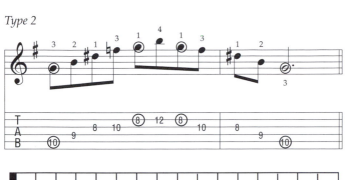

Type 2

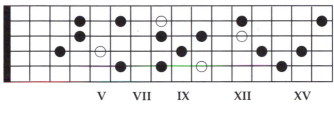

V   VII   IX   XII   XV

G

G7+

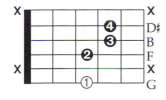

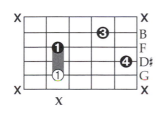

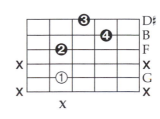

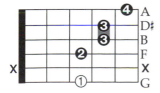

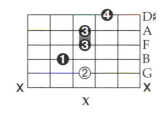

G9+

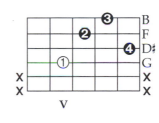

G pentatonic (major)

WWm3Wm3

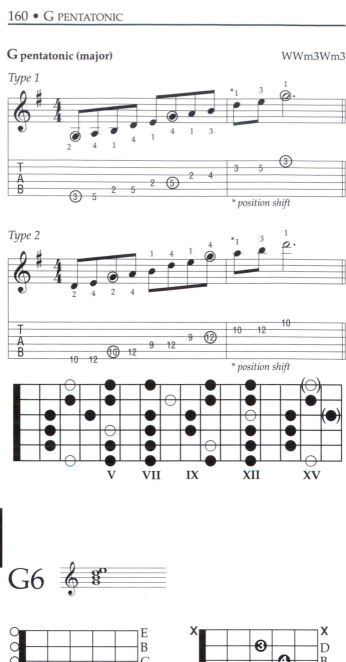

Type 1

* position shift

Type 2

* position shift

G

G6

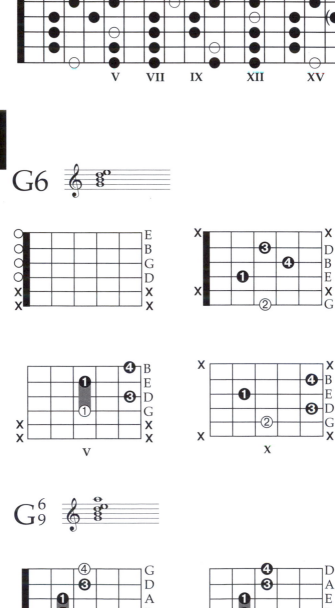

V

X

G 6/9

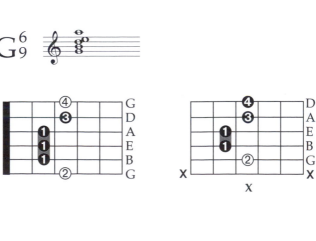

X

G6

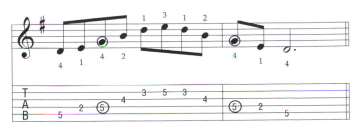

Type 1

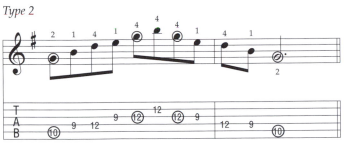

Type 2

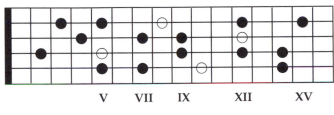

G

Gadd9

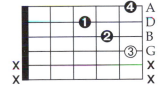
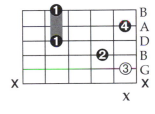

G pentatonic (minor)

m3WWm3W

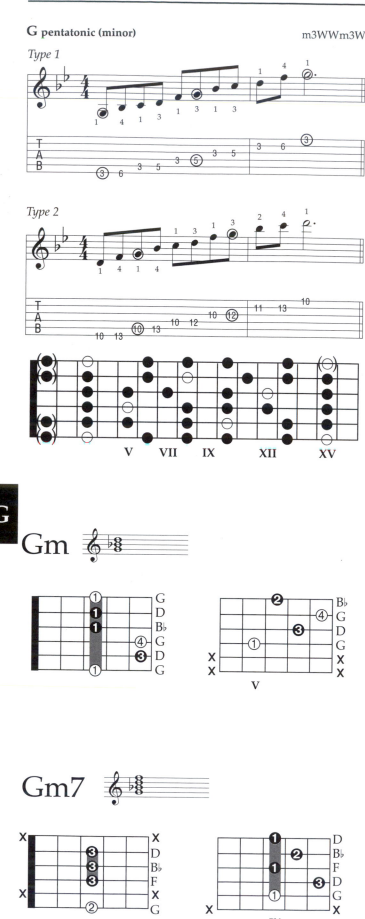

Gm7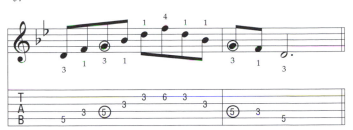

Type 1

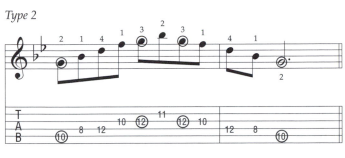

Type 2

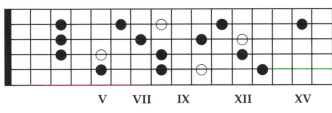

V   VII   IX   XII   XV

G

G7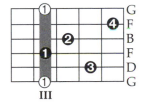

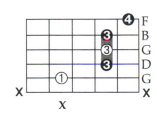

G7♯9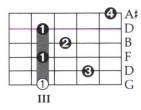

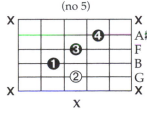

G blues scale (with major third & flatted fifth)   m3HHHHm3W

Type 1

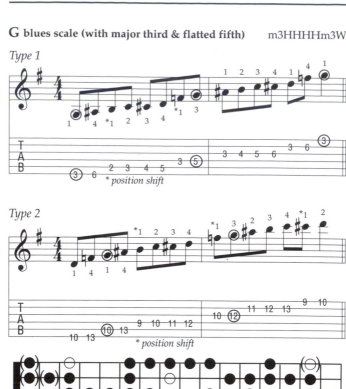

* position shift

Type 2

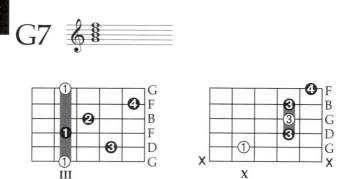

* position shift

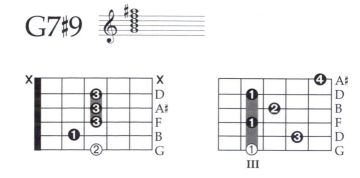

V   VII   IX   XII   XV

G

G7

```
III
```

G
F
B
F
D
G

X   X

F
B
G
D
G

G7♯9

X   X

D
A♯
F
B
G

```
III
```

A♯
D
B
F
D
G

G7♯9

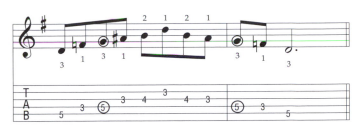

Type 1

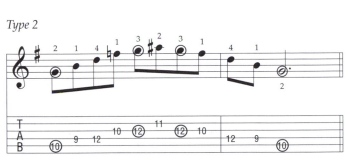

Type 2

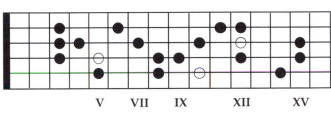

| V | VII | IX | XII | XV |

G9

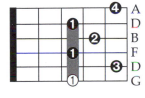

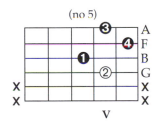

(no 5)

G13

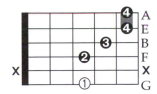

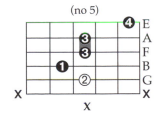

G

G diminished (whole-half)   WHWHWHWH

Type 1

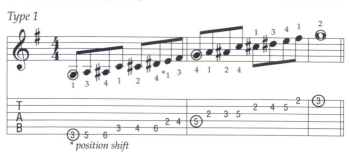

*position shift

Type 2

*position shift

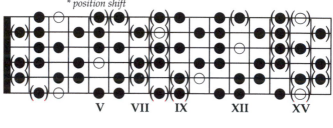

V   VII   IX   XII   XV

G

G°

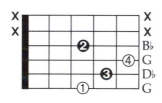

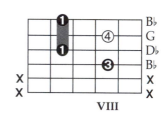

VIII

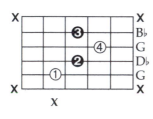

X

G°7

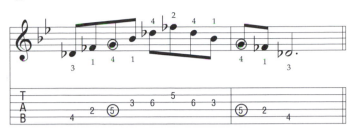

Type 1

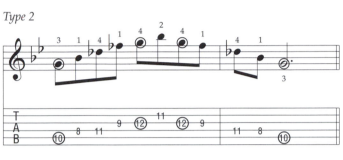

Type 2

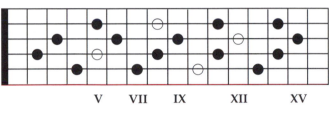

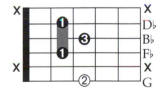

V   VII   IX   XII   XV

G

G°7

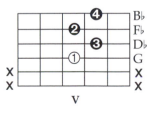

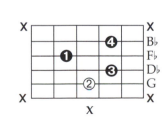

G#/A♭ major (Ionian)

WWHWWWH

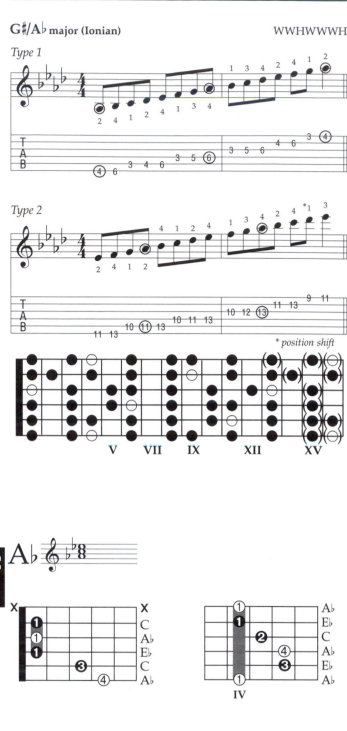

*position shift

A♭maj7

Type 1

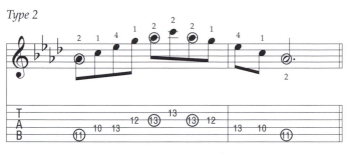

Type 2

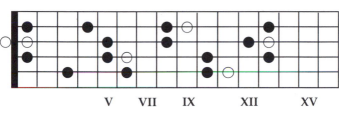

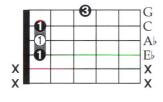

V VII IX XII XV

A♭maj7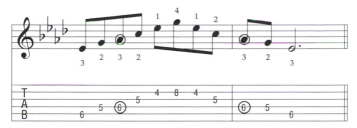

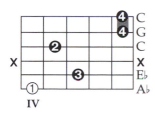

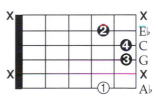

IV

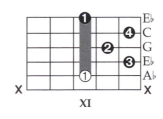

XI

G♯/A♭ natural minor (Aeolian)

WHWWHWW

Type 1

Type 2

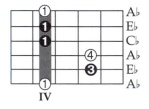

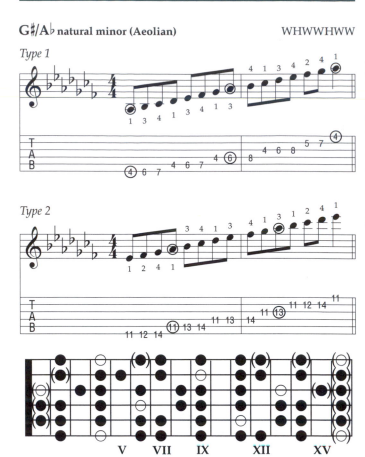

A♭m

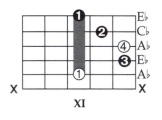

A♭m7

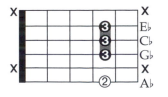
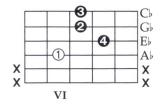

A♭m

Type 1

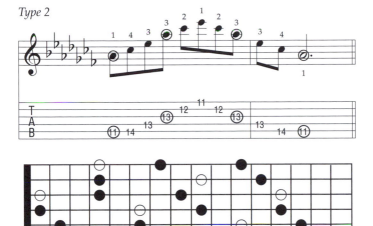

Type 2

A♭m add9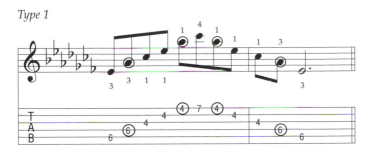

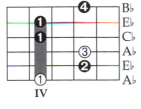

A♭m9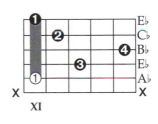

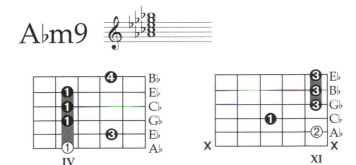

G♯
A♭

G#/A♭ harmonic minor

WHWWHm3H

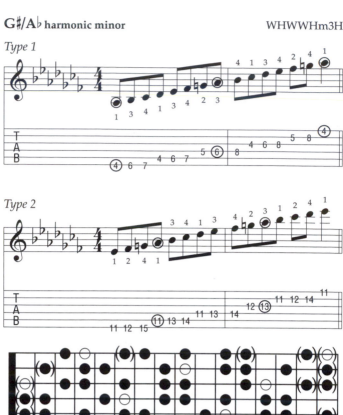

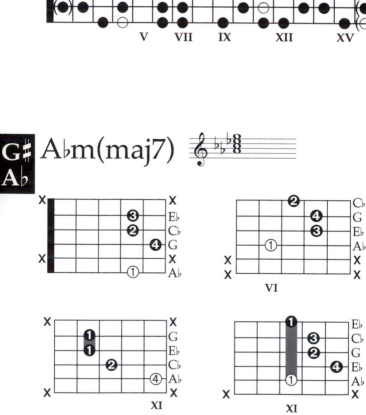

A♭m(maj7)

Type 1

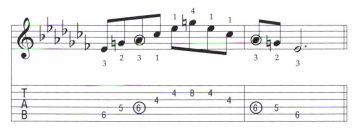

Type 2

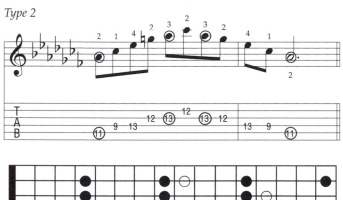

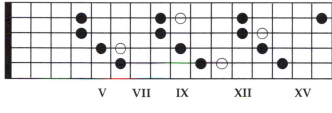

V   VII   IX   XII   XV

A♭m(maj9)

(no 5)

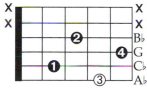

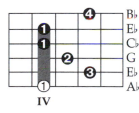

IV

(no 5)

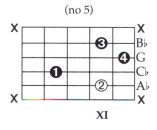

XI

G♯
A♭

G♯/A♭ jazz minor   WHWWWWH

Type 1

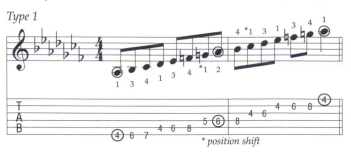

* position shift

Type 2

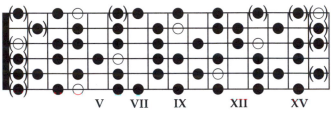

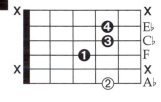

A♭m6

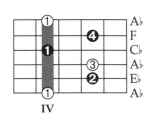

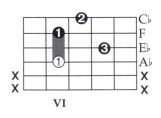

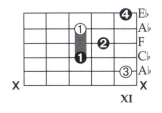

A♭m6

Type 1

Type 2

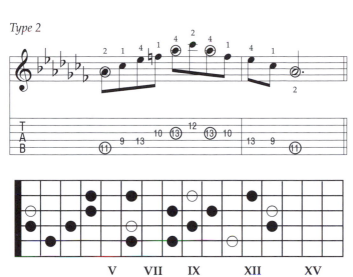

A♭m⁶₉

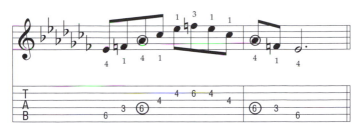

(no 5)

(no 5)

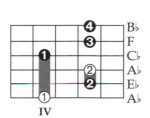

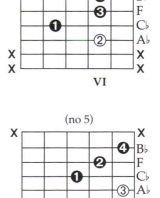

IV

XI

G♯/A♭ Mixolydian

WWHWWHW

Type 1

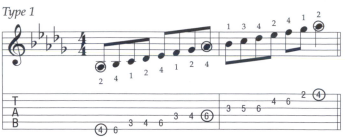

Type 2

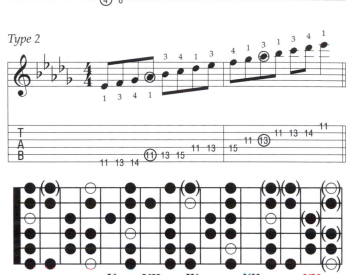

G♯ A♭

A♭7

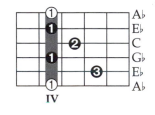

(no 5)

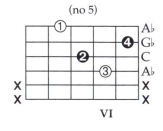

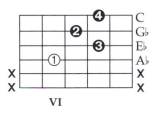

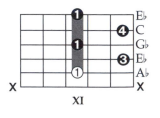

A♭7

Type 1

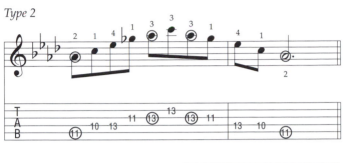

Type 2

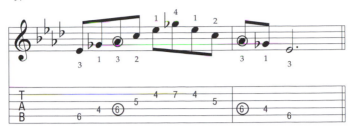

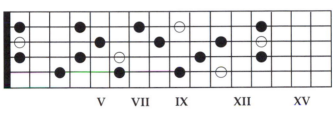

A♭9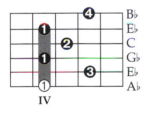

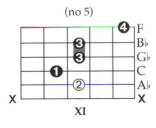

A♭13

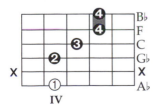

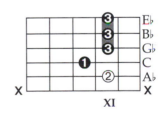

G♯/A♭ whole tone

WWWWWW

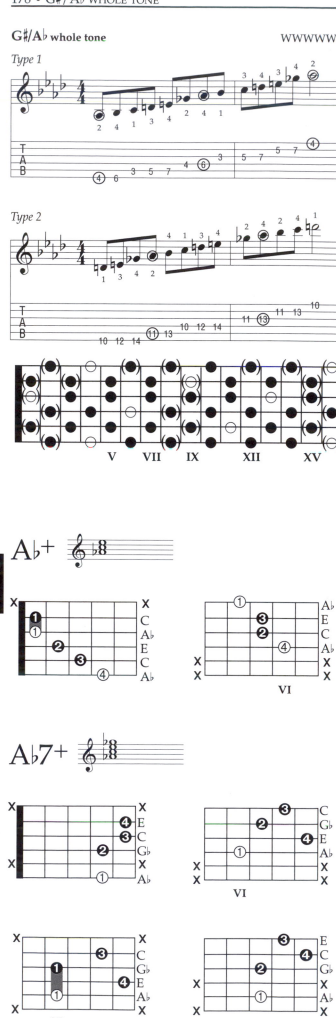

Type 1

Type 2

A♭+

A♭7+

VI

XI   XI

Ab7+

Type 1

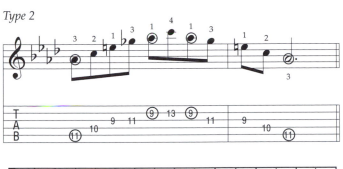

Type 2

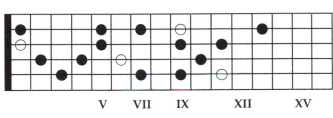

Ab7+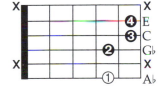

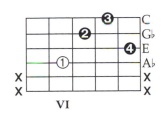

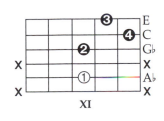

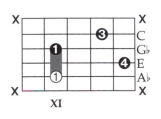

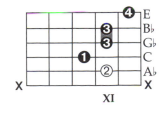

Ab9+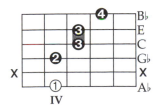

G#/A♭ pentatonic (major)

WWm3Wm3

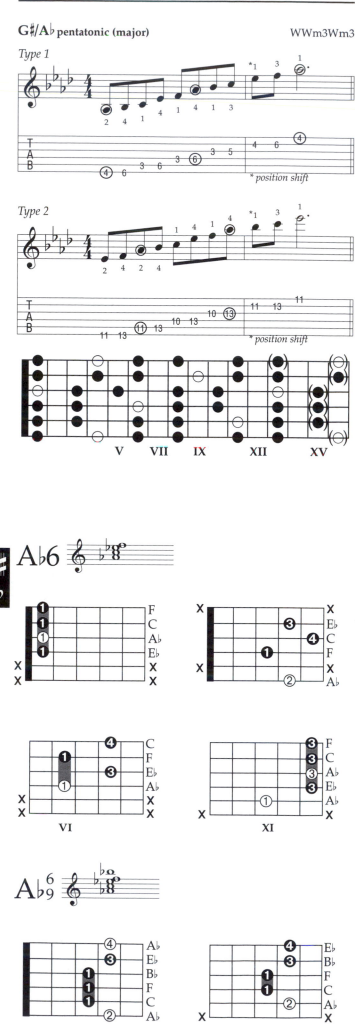

Type 1

* position shift

Type 2

* position shift

V   VII   IX   XII   XV

A♭6

VI   XI

A♭⁶₉

A♭6

Type 1

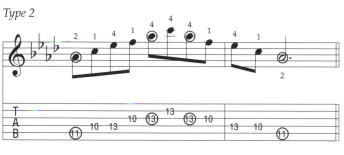

Type 2

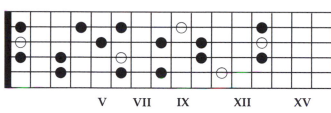

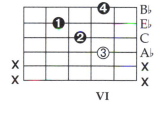

V   VII   IX   XII   XV

A♭add9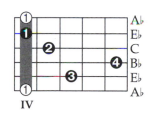

G♯
A♭

VI

IV

G♯/A♭ pentatonic (minor)

m3WWm3W

Type 1

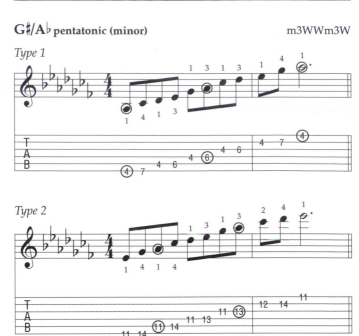

Type 2

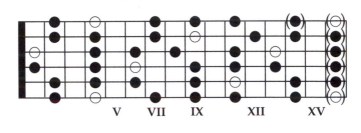

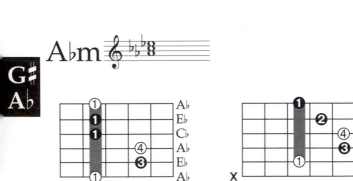

A♭m

A♭m7

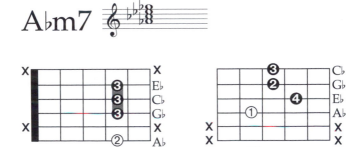

Abm7

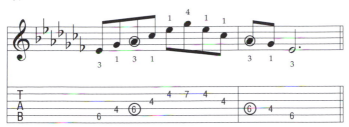

Type 1

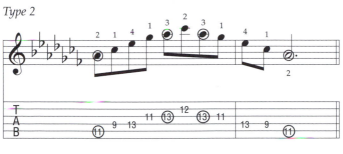

Type 2

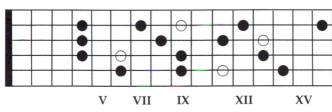

Ab7

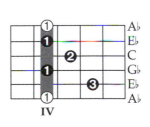

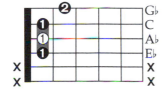

Ab7#9

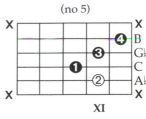

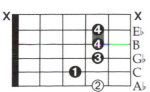

G#/A♭ blues scale (with major third & flatted fifth) m3HHHHm3W

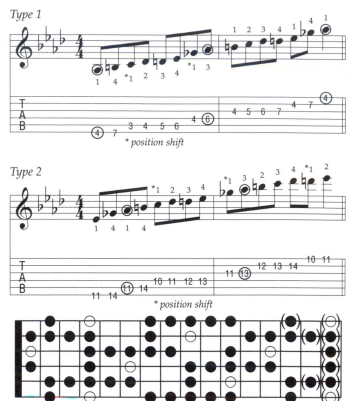

Type 1

Type 2

* position shift

A♭7

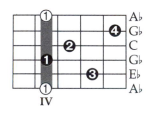

IV

XI

A♭7#9

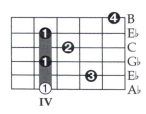

(no 5)

IV

XI

A♭7♯9

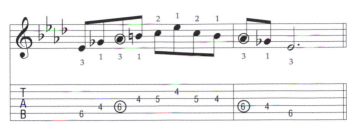

Type 1

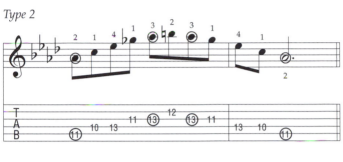

Type 2

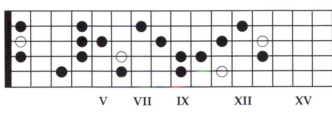

V   VII   IX   XII   XV

A♭9

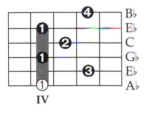

G♯
A♭

B♭	E♭
E♭	B♭
C	G♭
G♭	C
E♭	A♭
A♭	
IV	XI

A♭13

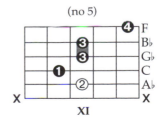

(no 5)

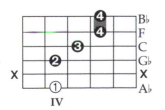
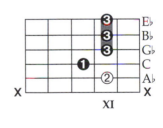

B♭	F
F	B♭
C	G♭
G♭	C
X	A♭
A♭	
IV	XI

G♯/A♭ diminished (whole-half)

WHWHWHWH

Type 1

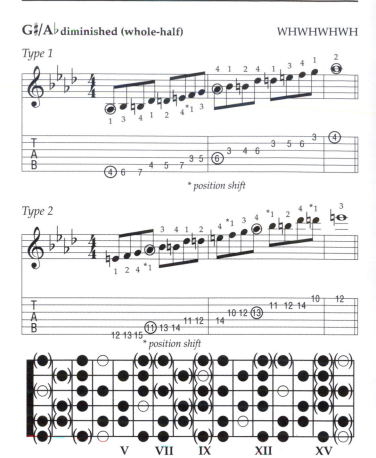

* position shift

Type 2

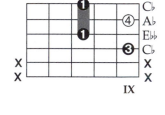

* position shift

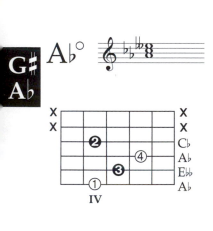

V   VII   IX   XII   XV

A♭°

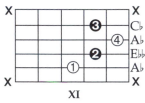

A♭°7

Type 1

Type 2

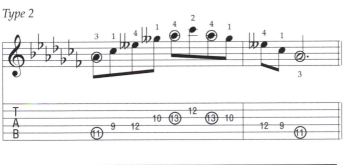

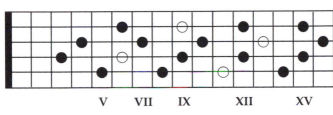

V   VII   IX   XII   XV

A♭°7

G♯
A♭

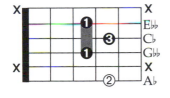

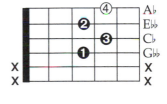

X — E♭♭ / C♭ / G♭♭ / X — A♭

A♭ / E♭♭ / C♭ / G♭♭ / X / X

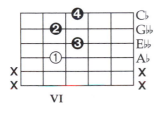

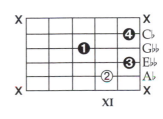

C♭ / G♭♭ / E♭♭ / A♭ / X / X

VI

X — C♭ / G♭♭ / E♭♭ / A♭ / X

XI

A major (Ionian)

WWHWWWH

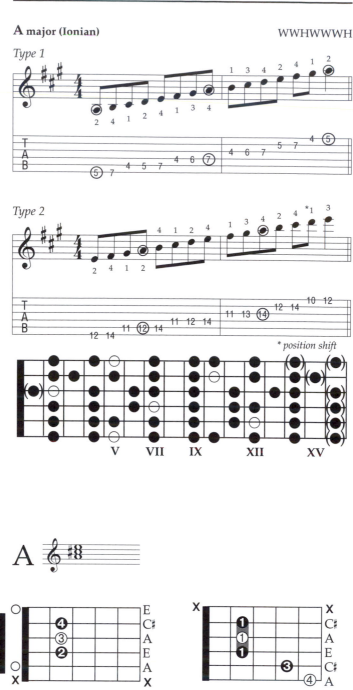

*position shift

A

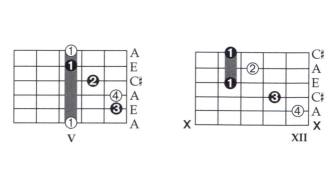

Amaj7
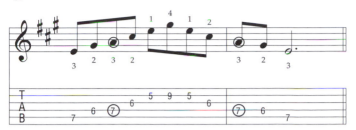

Type 1

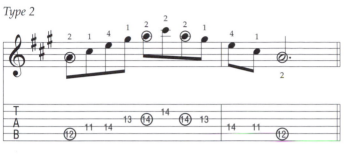

Type 2

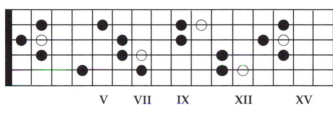

Amaj7

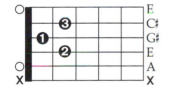

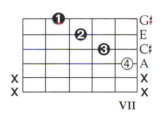

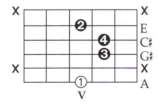

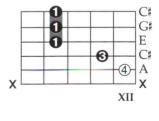

A

A natural minor (Aeolian)

WHWWHWW

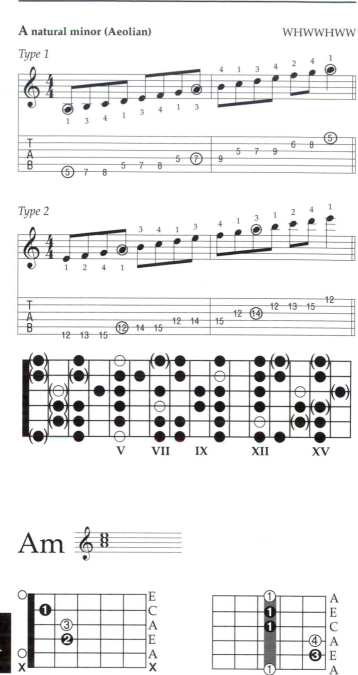

Am

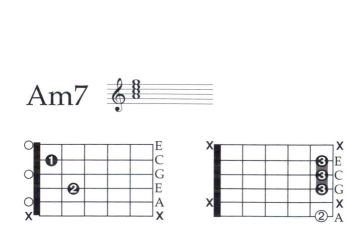

Am

Type 1

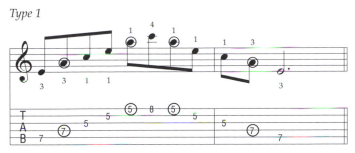

Type 2

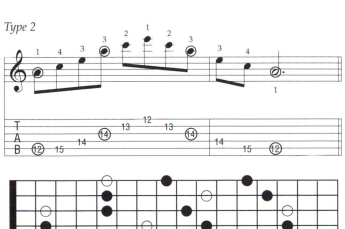

V   VII   IX   XII   XV

Am add9

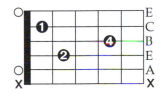

A

Am9

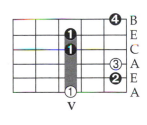

(no 5)

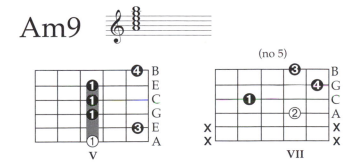

V   VII

A harmonic minor

WHWWHm3H

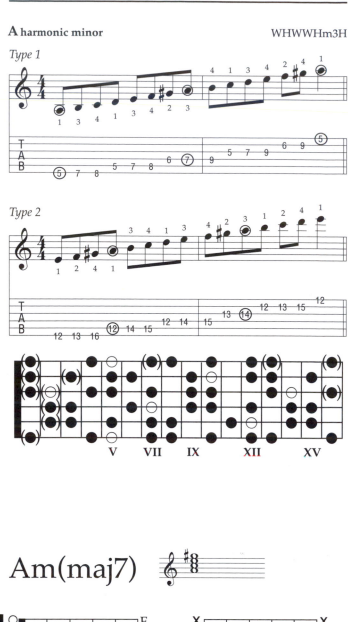

Am(maj7)

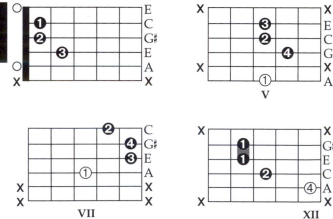

Am(maj7)

Type 1

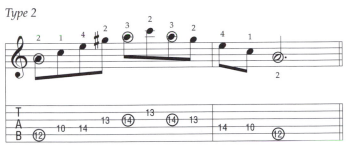

Type 2

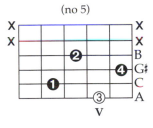

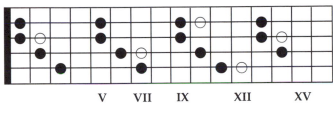

Am(maj9)

(no 5)

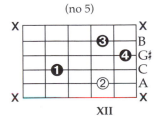

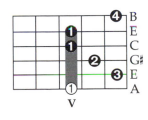

(no 5)

A jazz minor WHWWWWH

Type 1

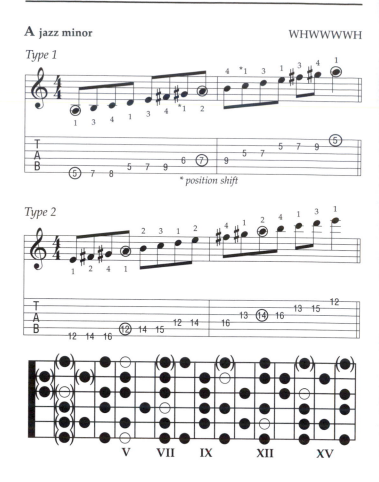

* position shift

Type 2

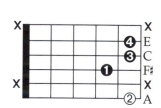

Am6

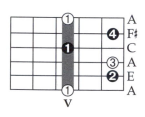

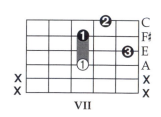

Am6

Type 1

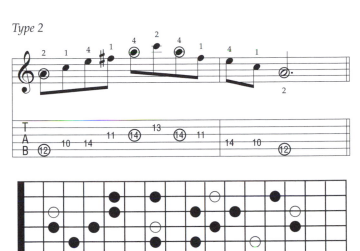

Type 2

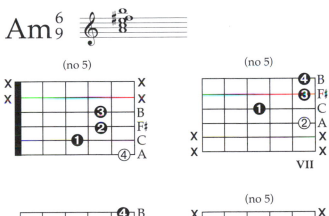

| | V | VII | IX | XII | XV |

Am$^6_9$

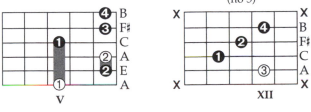

A Mixolydian   WWHWWHW

Type 1

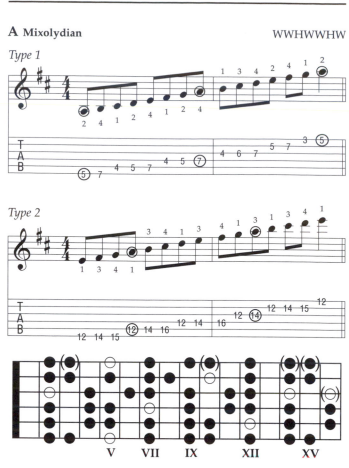

Type 2

A7

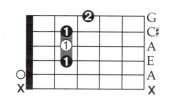

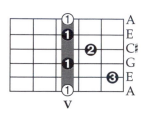

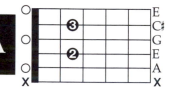

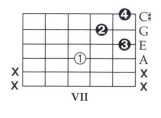

A7

Type 1

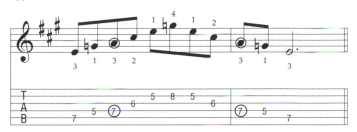

Type 2

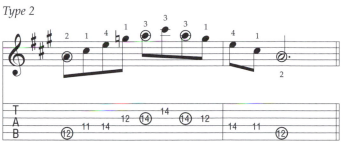

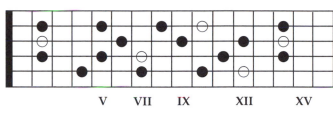

V	VII	IX	XII	XV

A9

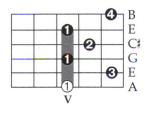

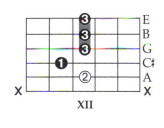

A

A13

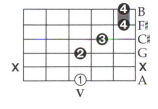

(no 5)

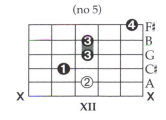

A whole tone

WWWWWW

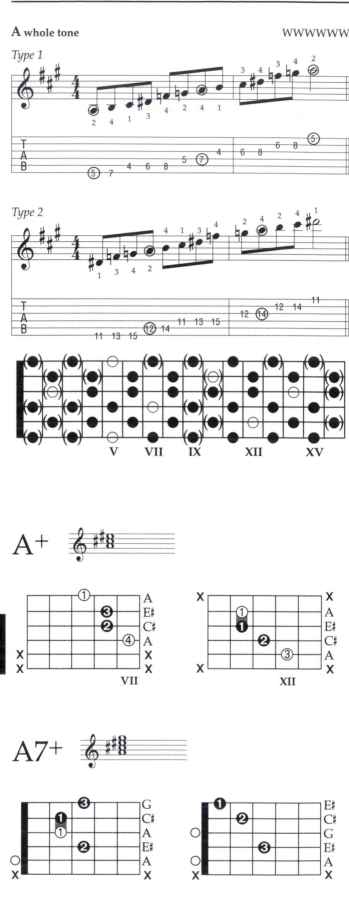

A+

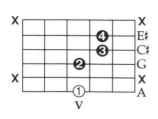

A7+

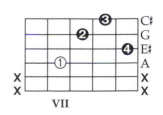

A7+

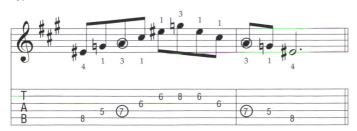

Type 1

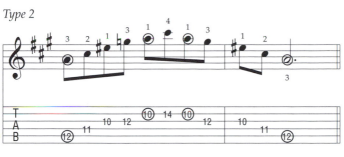

Type 2

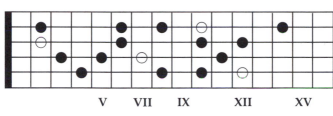

A7+

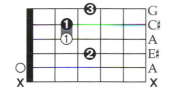

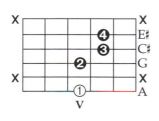

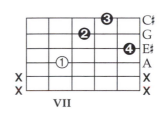

A9+

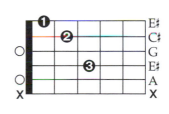

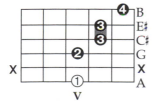

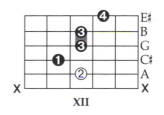

A

A pentatonic (major)

WWm3Wm3

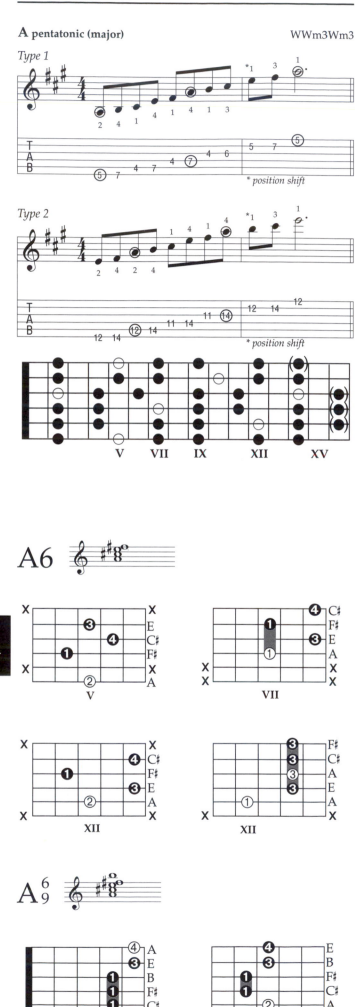

Type 1

* *position shift*

Type 2

* *position shift*

V   VII   IX   XII   XV

A6

A$^6_9$

A6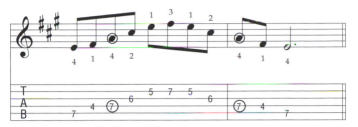

Type 1

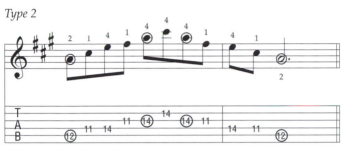

Type 2

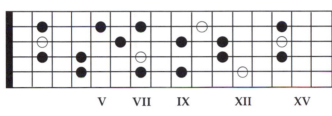

Aadd9

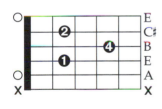

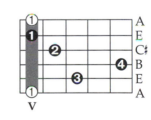

A

A pentatonic (minor)

m3WWm3W

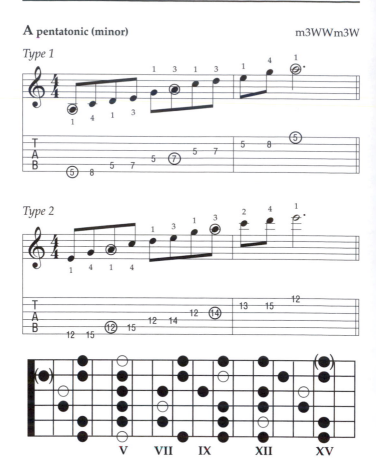

Type 1

Type 2

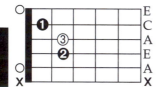

Am

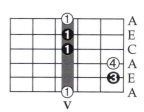

Am7

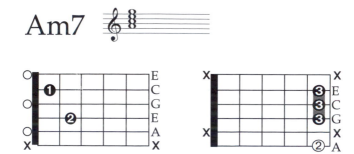

Am7

Type 1

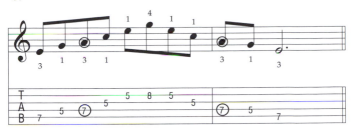

Type 2

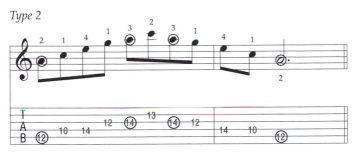

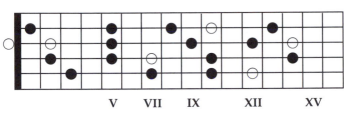

A7

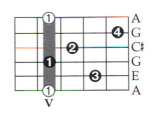

A7♯9

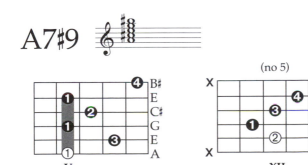

A blues scale (with major third & flatted fifth)   m3HHHHm3W

Type 1

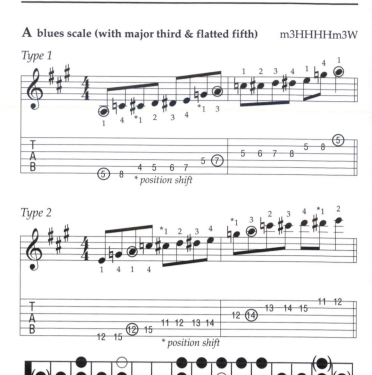

*position shift

Type 2

*position shift

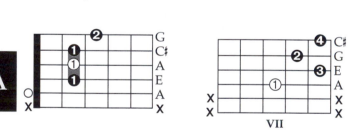

V   VII   IX   XII   XV

A7

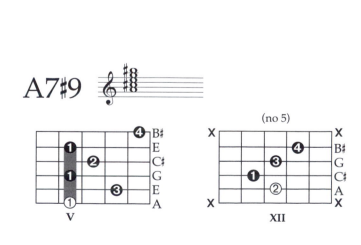

A7♯9

A7♯9

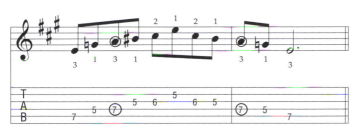

Type 1

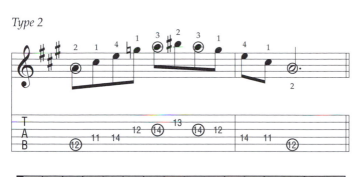

Type 2

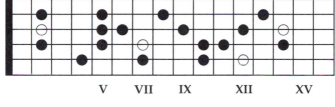

A9

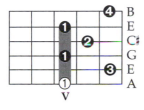

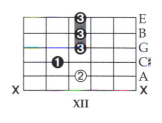

A13

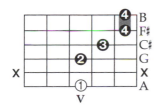

(no 5)

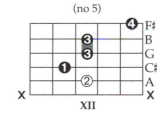

A diminished (whole-half)

WHWHWHWH

Type 1

* position shift

Type 2

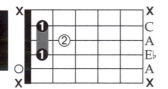

* position shift

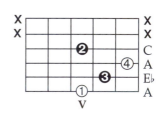

V   VII   IX   XII   XV

A°

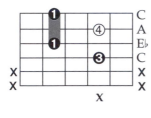

A°7

Type 1

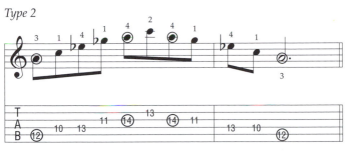

Type 2

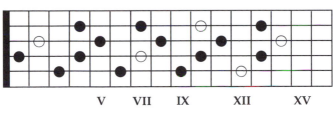

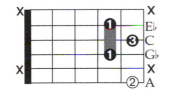

A°7

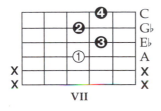

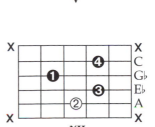

A#/B♭ major (Ionian)

WWHWWWH

Type 1

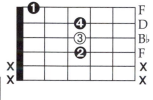

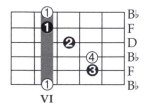

Type 2

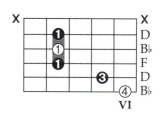

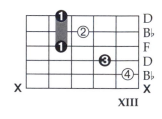

* position shift

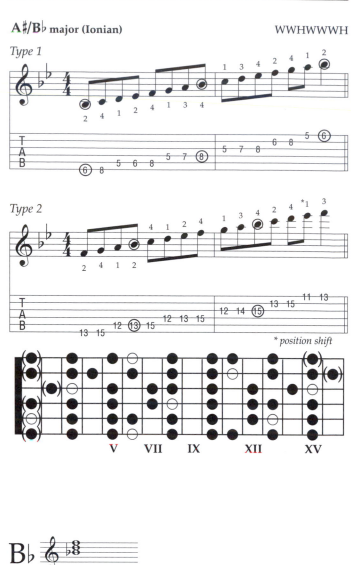

V   VII   IX   XII   XV

B♭maj7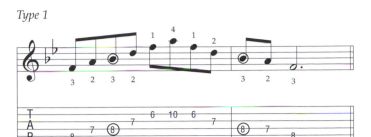

Type 1

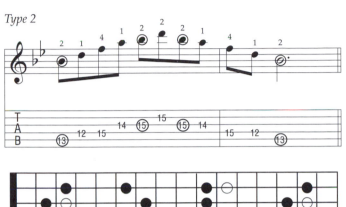

Type 2

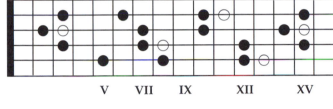

B♭maj7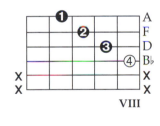

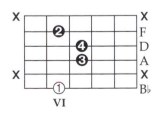

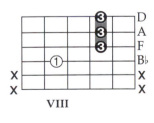

A♯/B♭ natural minor (Aeolian)

WHWWHWW

Type 1

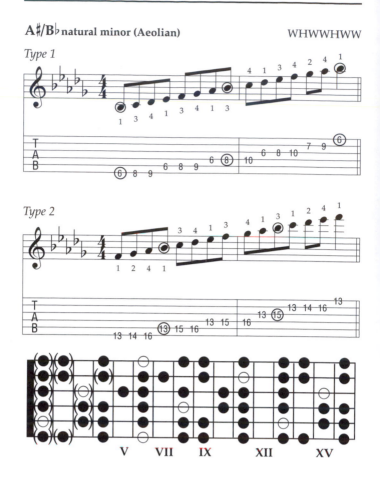

Type 2

B♭m

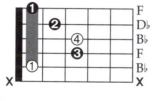

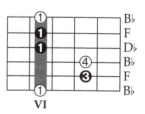

B♭m7

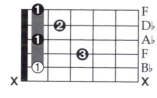

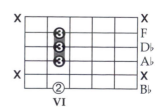

B♭m

Type 1

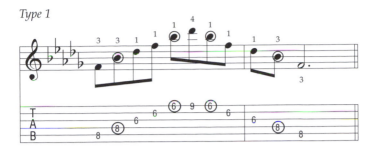

Type 2

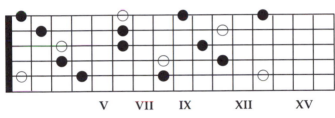

| V | VII | IX | XII | XV |

B♭m add9

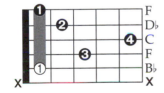

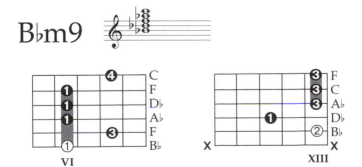

F
D♭
C
F
B♭

B♭
F
D♭
C
F
B♭

VI

A♯
B♭

B♭m9

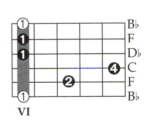

C
F
D♭
A♭
F
B♭

VI

F
C
A♭
D♭
B♭

XIII

A#/B♭ harmonic minor

WHWWHm3H

Type 1

Type 2

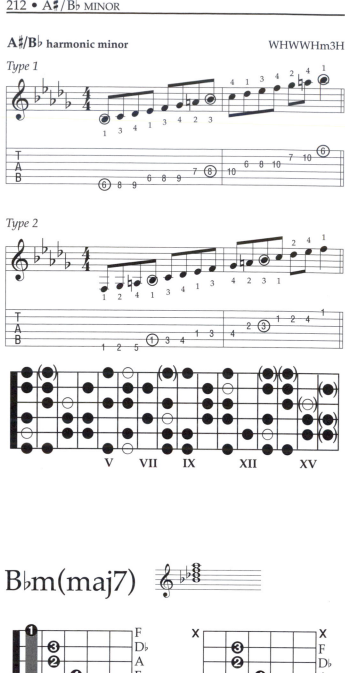

B♭m(maj7)

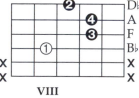

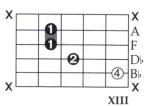

VI

VIII

XIII

B♭m(maj7)

Type 1

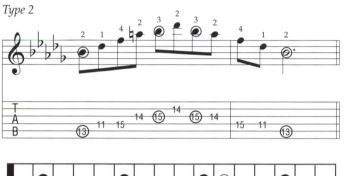

Type 2

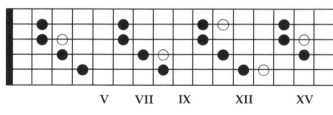

| V | VII | IX | XII | XV |

B♭m(maj9)

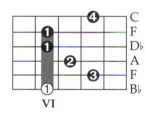

(no 5)

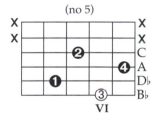

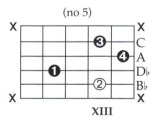

(no 5)

XIII

A♯
B♭

A#/B♭ jazz minor

WHWWWWH

Type 1

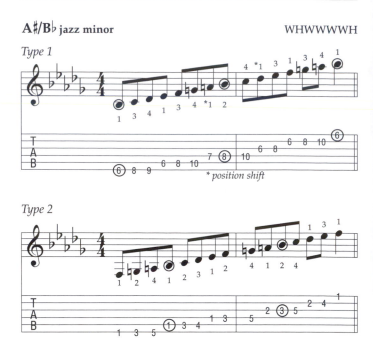

* position shift

Type 2

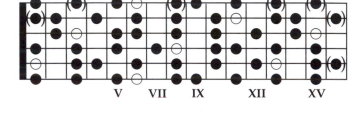

V   VII   IX   XII   XV

B♭m6

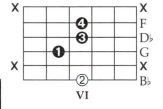

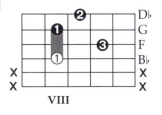

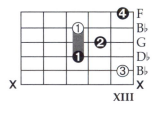

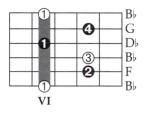

B♭m6

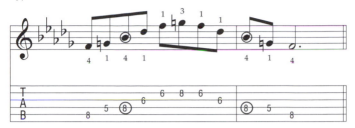

Type 1

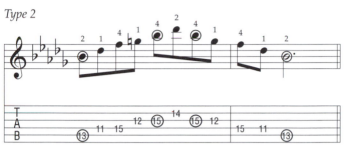

Type 2

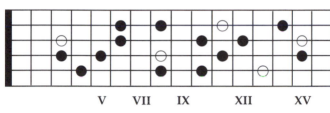

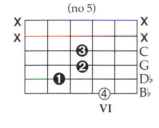

V   VII   IX   XII   XV

B♭m$\frac{6}{9}$

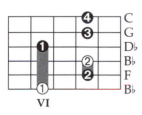

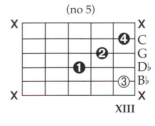

(no 5)

VI

(no 5)

VIII

VI

(no 5)

XIII

A♯/B♭ Mixolydian

WWHWWHW

Type 1

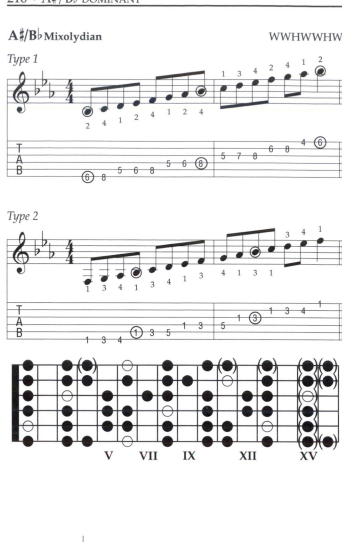

Type 2

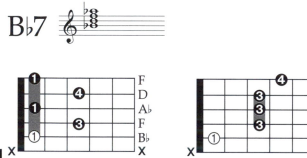

B♭7

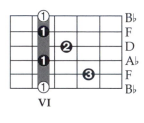

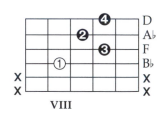

Bb7

Type 1

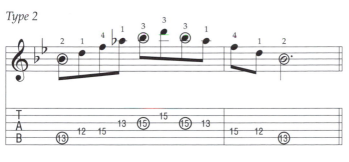

Type 2

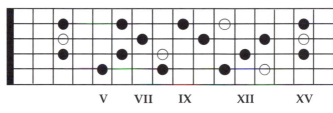

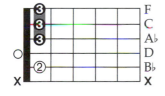

V   VII   IX   XII   XV

Bb9

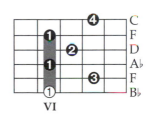

Bb13

(no 5)

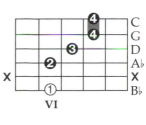

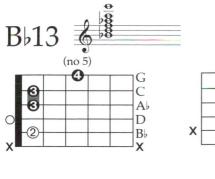

A♯/B♭ whole tone

WWWWWW

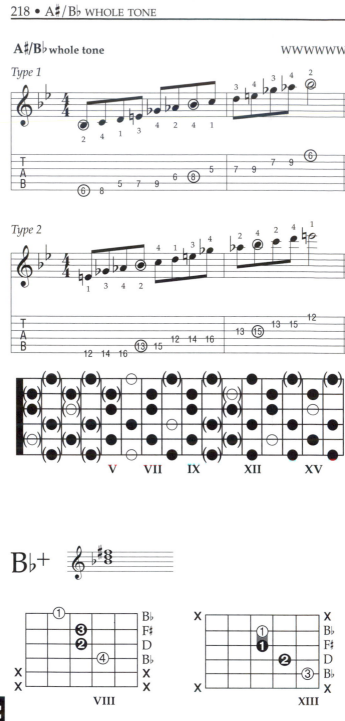

Type 1

Type 2

A♯
B♭

B♭+

B♭7+

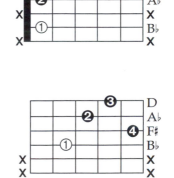

B♭7+

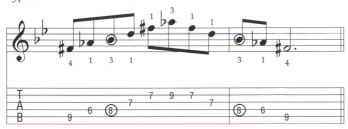

Type 1

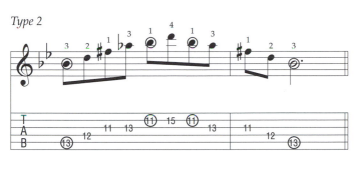

Type 2

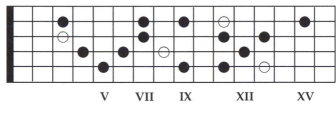

B♭7+

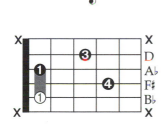

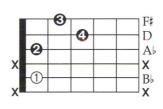

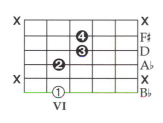

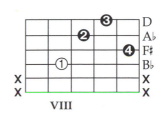

A♯ / B♭

B♭9+

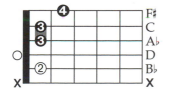

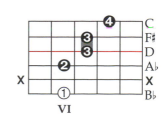

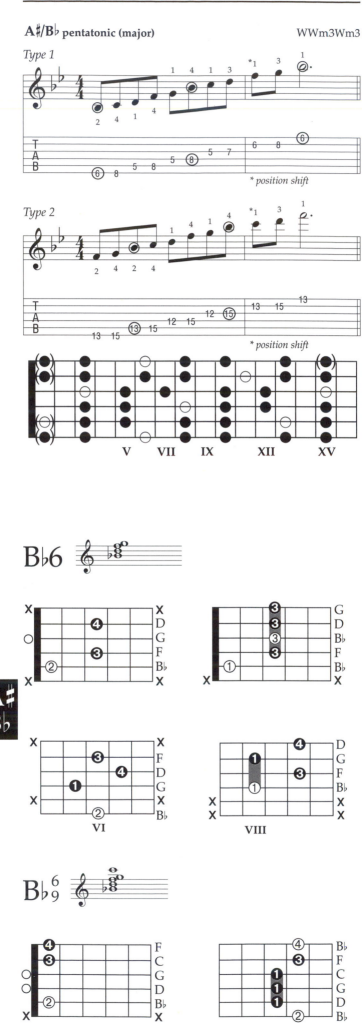

A#/B♭ pentatonic (major) WWm3Wm3

Type 1

* position shift

Type 2

* position shift

V   VII   IX   XII   XV

B♭6

VI   VIII

B♭9/6

B♭6

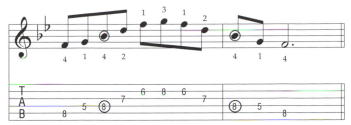

Type 1

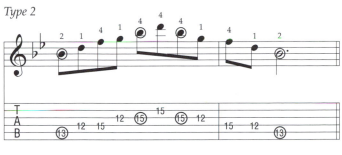

Type 2

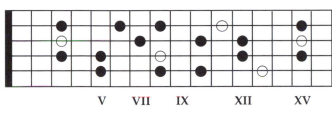

B♭add9

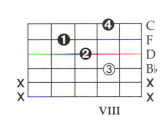

A♯/B♭ pentatonic (minor)

m3WWm3W

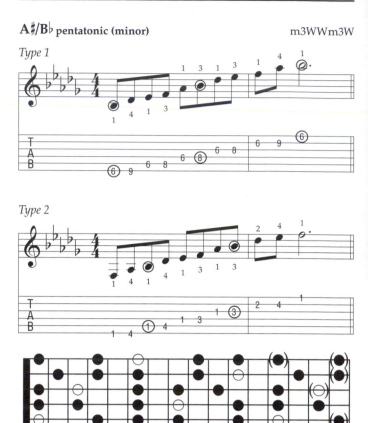

Type 1

Type 2

V   VII   IX   XII   XV

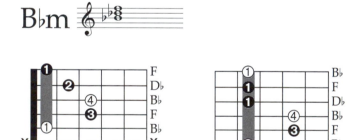

B♭m

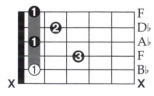

F
D♭
B♭
F
B♭

B♭
F
D♭
B♭
F
B♭

VI

B♭m7

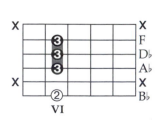

F
D♭
A♭
F
B♭

F
D♭
A♭
B♭

VI

A♯
B♭

B♭m7

Type 1

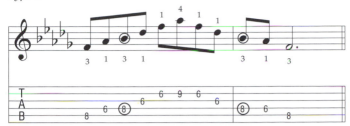

Type 2

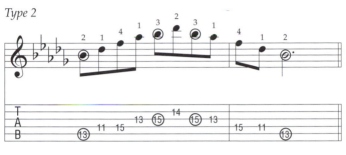

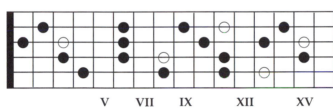

| | V | VII | IX | XII | XV |

B♭7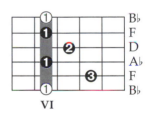

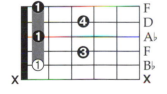

F
D
A♭
F
B♭

X   X

B♭
F
D
A♭
F
B♭

VI

A♯
B♭

B♭7♯9

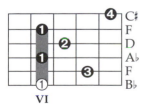

C♯
F
D
A♭
F
B♭

VI

(no 5)

X   X

X   X

C
A♭
D
B♭

XIII

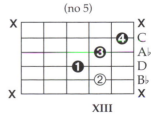

A♯/B♭ blues scale (with major third & flatted fifth) m3HHHHm3W

Type 1

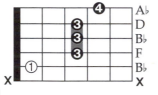

* position shift

Type 2

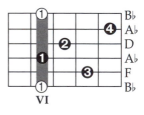

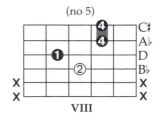

* position shift

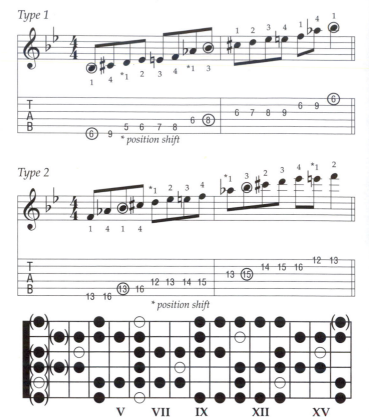

V   VII   IX   XII   XV

B♭7

B♭7♯9

B♭7♯9

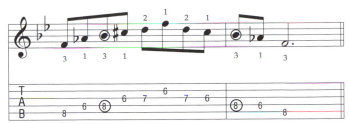

Type 1

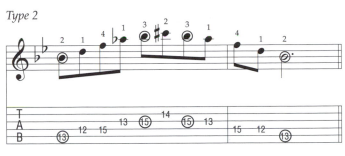

Type 2

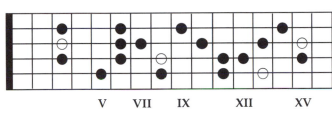

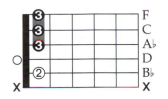

V   VII   IX   XII   XV

B♭9

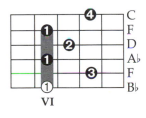

B♭13

(no 5)

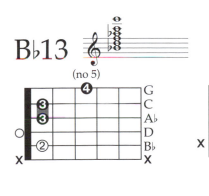

A♯/B♭ diminished (whole-half)

WHWHWHWH

Type 1

* position shift

Type 2

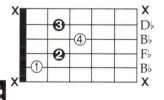

* position shift

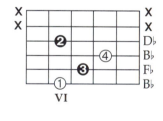

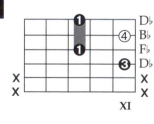

B♭°

B♭°7

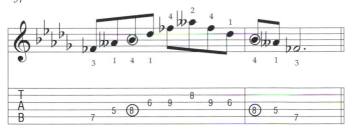

Type 1

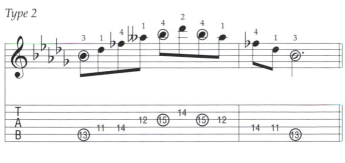

Type 2

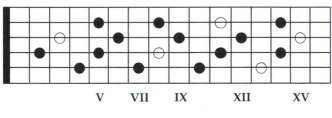

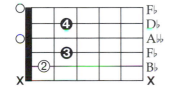

| V | VII | IX | XII | XV |

B♭°7

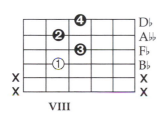

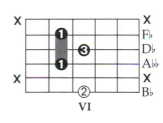

VI

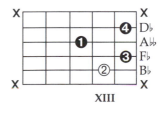

VIII

XIII

A♯
B♭

B major (Ionian)

WWHWWWH

Type 1

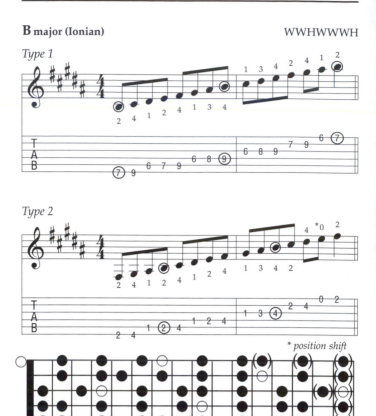

Type 2

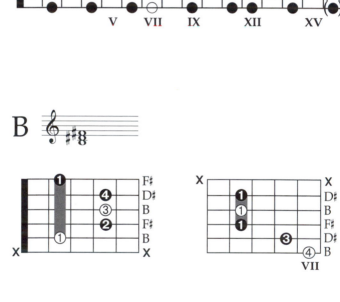

* *position shift*

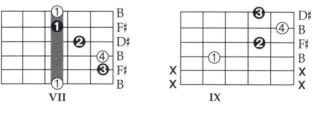

B

Bmaj7

Type 1

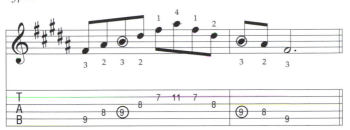

Type 2

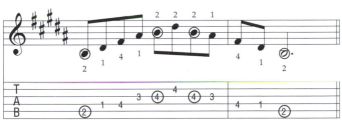

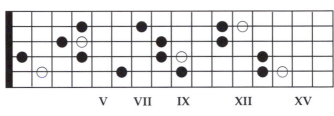

V   VII   IX   XII   XV

Bmaj7

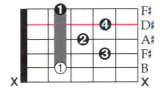

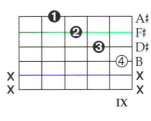

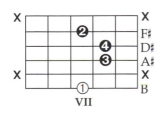

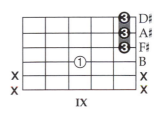

B

B natural minor (Aeolian)   WHWWHWW

Type 1

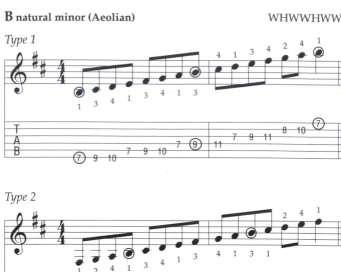

Type 2

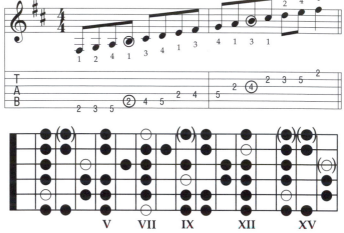

Bm

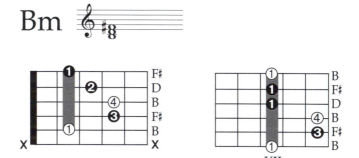

B

Bm7

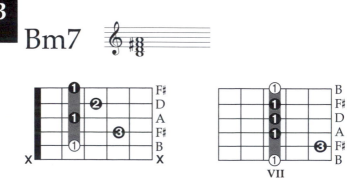

Bm

Type 1

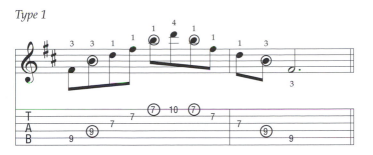

Type 2

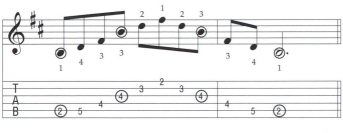

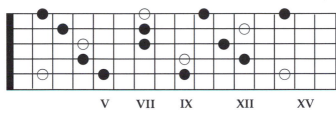

V   VII   IX   XII   XV

Bm add9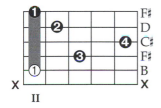

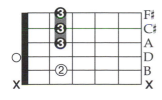

II

F#
D
C#
F#
B

VII

C#
F#
D
B
F#
B

B

Bm9

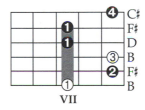

F#
C#
A
D
B

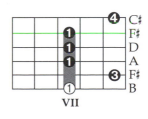

C#
F#
D
A
F#
B

VII

B harmonic minor

WHWWHm3H

Bm(maj7)

Bm(maj7)

Type 1

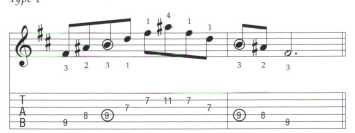

Type 2

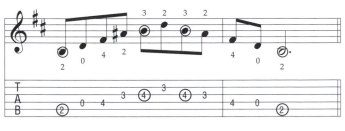

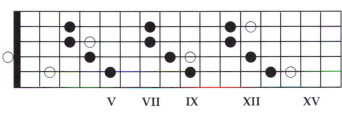

V   VII   IX   XII   XV

Bm(maj9)

(no 5)

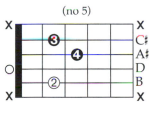

(no 5)

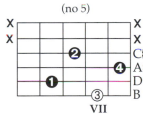

VII

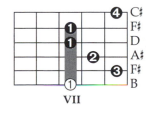

VII

B

B jazz minor WHWWWWH

Type 1

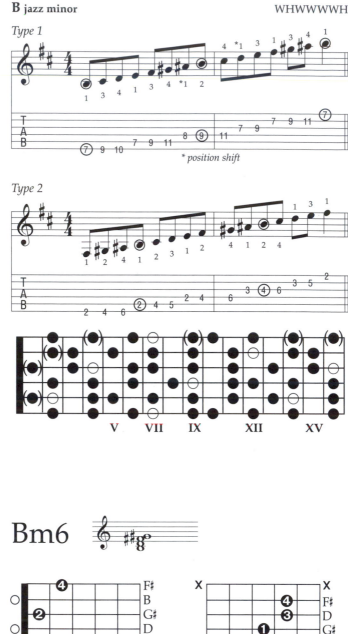

* position shift

Type 2

V VII IX XII XV

Bm6

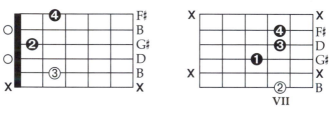

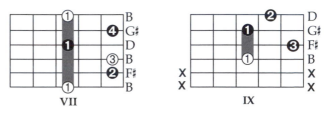

Bm6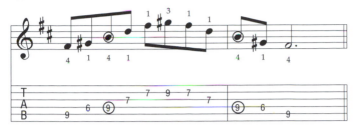

Type 1

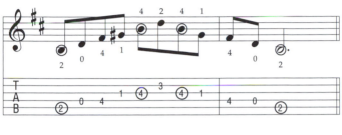

Type 2

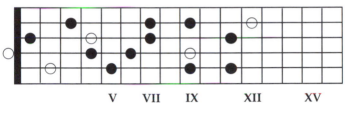

| V | VII | IX | XII | XV |

Bm $^6_9$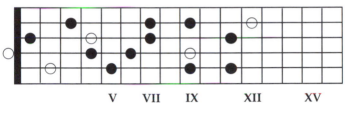

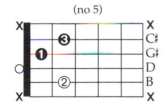

(no 5)

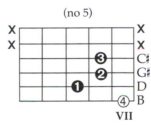

(no 5)

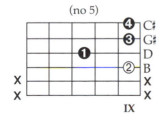

(no 5)

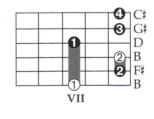

B

B Mixolydian   WWHWWHW

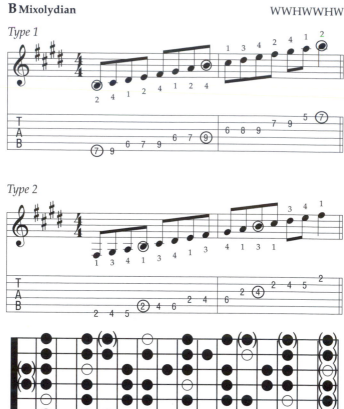

Type 1

Type 2

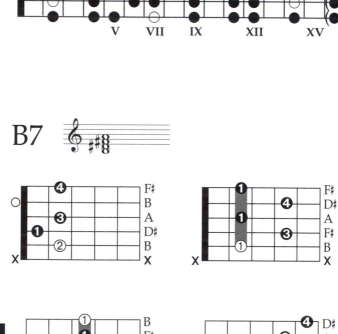

V   VII   IX   XII   XV

B7

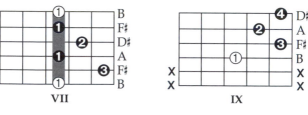

VII   IX

B7

Type 1

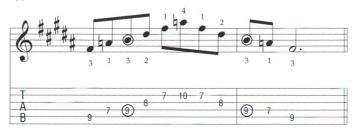

Type 2

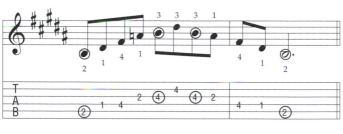

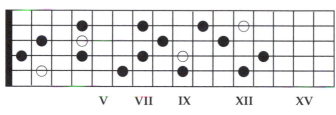

V   VII   IX   XII   XV

B9

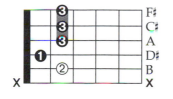

(no 5)

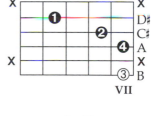

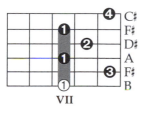

VII

(no 5)

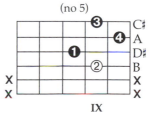

IX

B13

(no 5)

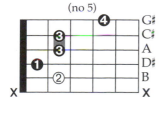

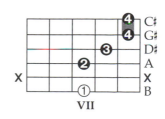

VII

B whole tone   WWWWWW

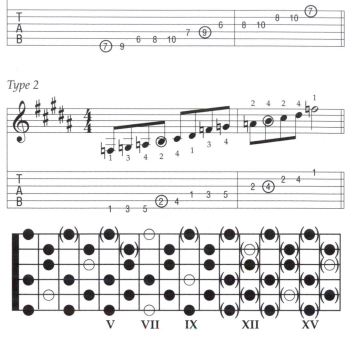

B+

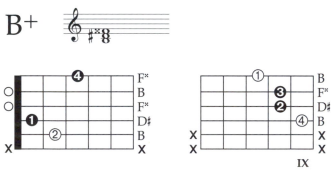

B7+

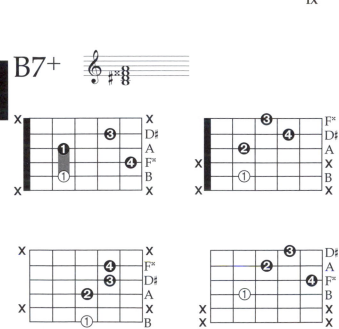

B7+

Type 1

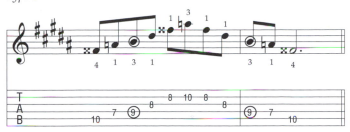

Type 2

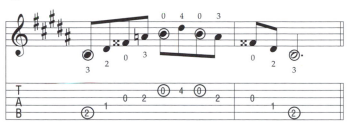

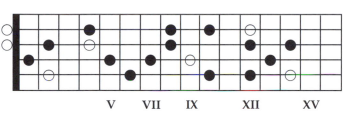

| | V | VII | IX | XII | XV |

B7+

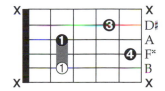
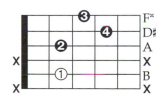

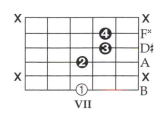
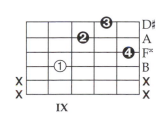

B

B9+

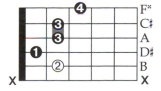
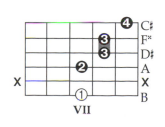

B pentatonic (major)

WWm3Wm3

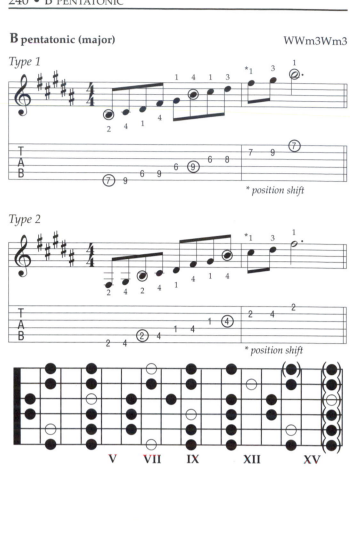

Type 1

* position shift

Type 2

* position shift

B6

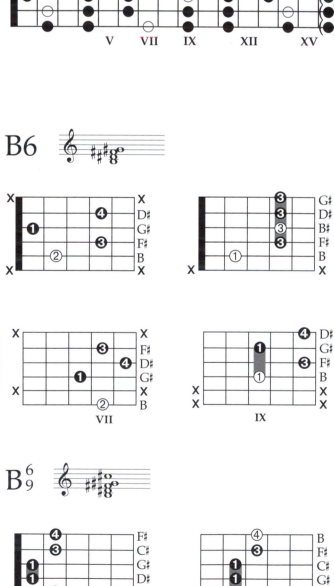

X X D# G# F# B X

G# D# B# F#
B

X F# D# G# X B
VII

D# G# F# B X X
IX

B⁶₉

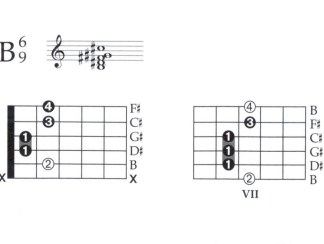

F# C# G# D# B
X X

B F# C# G# D# B
VII

B6

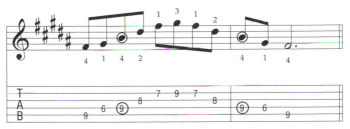

Type 1

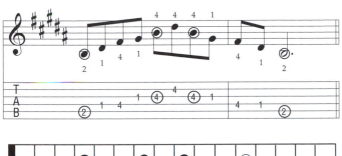

Type 2

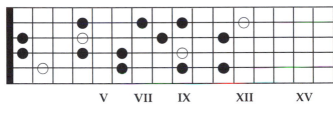

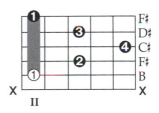

V   VII   IX   XII   XV

Badd9

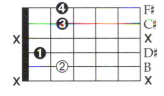

B

B pentatonic (minor)

m3WWm3W

Type 1

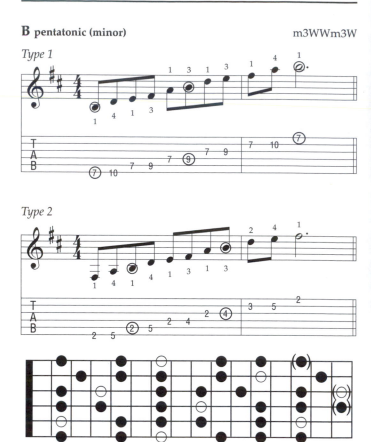

Type 2

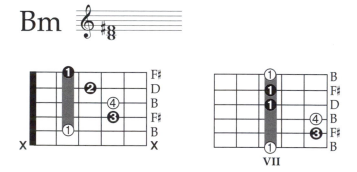

Bm

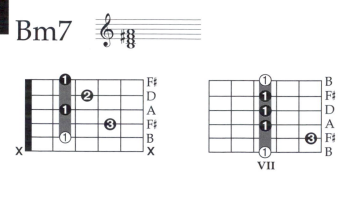

B

Bm7

Bm7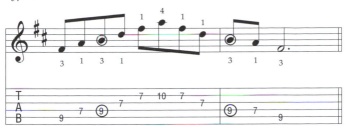

Type 1

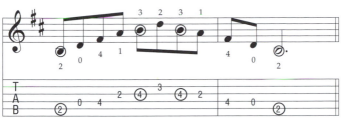

Type 2

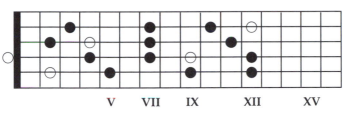

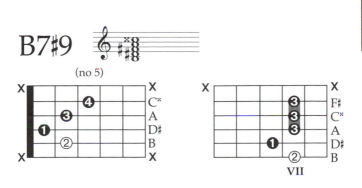

| | V | VII | IX | XII | XV |

B7

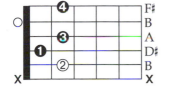

B

B7♯9

(no 5)

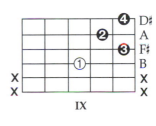

B blues scale (with major third & flatted fifth)   m3HHHHm3W

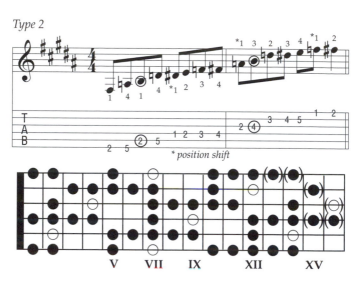

Type 1

Type 2

* position shift

* position shift

B7

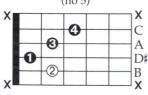

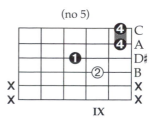

VII

B

B7♯9

(no 5)   (no 5)

IX

B7♯9

Type 1

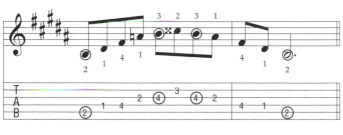

Type 2

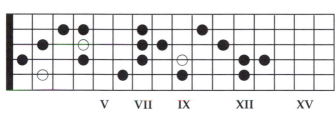

V   VII   IX   XII   XV

B9

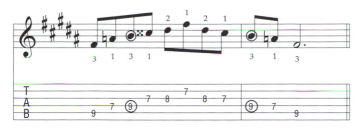

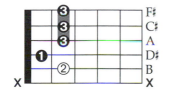

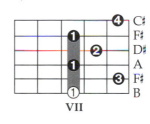

B13

(no 5)

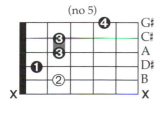

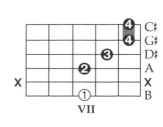

B

B diminished (whole-half)   WHWHWHWH

Type 1

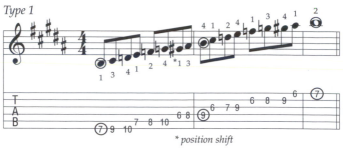

* position shift

Type 2

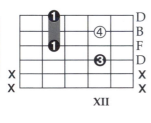

* position shift

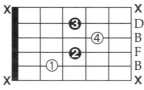

V   VII   IX   XII   XV

B°

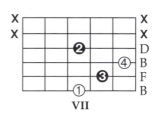

VII

XII

B

B°7

Type 1

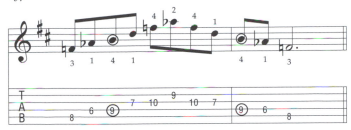

Type 2

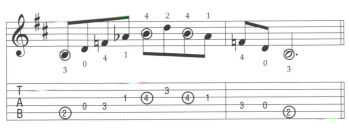

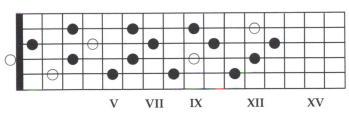

| | V | VII | IX | XII | XV |

B°7

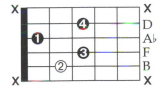

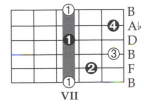

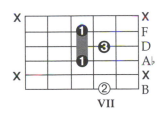

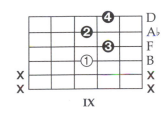

B

Gig Bag Book Of...

From The **Music Sales** Group

- Fits right in your instrument case!
- Packed with information right at your fingertips!
- Full of diagrams and clear, close-up photos